ba **D0453191** rs

Printed in the United Kingdom by MPG Books Ltd, Bodmin

Published in the UK by SMT, an imprint of Sanctuary Publishing Limited,
Sanctuary House, 45-53 Sinclair Road, London W14 0NS, United Kingdom

www.sanctuarypublishing.com

ISBN: 1-86074-266-1

basic Mixers

Paul White

smt

Also by Paul White and available from Sanctuary Publishing:

Also by Paul White in this series:

CONTENTS

INTRODUCTION

No matter if you record using a traditional hardware-based studio, record using a computer or record live sound, you need to know how mixing consoles work. Today mixers may be analogue, digital or virtual (ie they exist only inside a computer), but they all follow a similar underlying logic, so if you know how the traditional analogue console works you should soon be able to find your way around its digital equivalent.

Newcomers to recording are often a little intimidated by the control surface of a studio mixer – all those knobs and faders! – but it's all a lot easier to understand than it might at first appear. By approaching the basic concepts of mixers in simple stages, you'll be able to find your way around virtually any recording or live sound console in a very short space of time.

As with the other books in this series, the aim is to go into as much detail as possible while keeping the explanations clear and straightforward. It took me many years to learn everything that's in this book, but I'd like to pass it on so that others involved in recording music can achieve their full creative potential in considerably less time than it took me.

1 THE MIXING CONSOLE

The mixing console, whether in the studio or on stage, is the nerve centre of the audio system. It's from here that everything is controlled, and it's into the mixer that external signal processing devices, such as compressors, gates and reverb units, are plugged. The best way to familiarise yourself with mixers is to examine the purpose and structure of a typical analogue mixer. Even if you're using a digital mixer, or the virtual mixer built into an audio/MIDI software sequencing package, the analogue model of signal routing is still the best place to start.

Many people find the complexity of a full-size studio or live sound console daunting at first – have you noticed how the first thing an outsider does is look at the mixer and ask you how on earth you know what all the knobs do? Even if you've used a basic 'live' sound console before, the extra routing functions of a recording mixer may still be confusing at first sight. However, it all falls into place quite quickly as long as you approach things logically and don't expect to master everything at once. To start right at the beginning, what does a mixer do, and why we need it? In fact a mixer does several jobs at once: it changes the levels of different signals; it combines signals; it routes signals to different destinations, such as tape machine inputs, power amplifiers, effects units and so on; and it also provides a degree of signal processing by way of its equalisers. The first thing to look at is the need to change the level of a signal.

The Need For Gain

All analogue circuitry, including that used in mixers, has an optimum operating range that provides the best noise performance and the lowest distortion. If the input signal exceeds this range, distortion will result, while if the signal falls too far below it, the amount of amplification required to bring it back up to a usable level will also make it noisy. Equivalent constraints apply within digital systems, but understanding the analogue world is most useful at this point. Most analogue audio circuitry is designed to work within a particular range of signal levels, usually up to around 10v, so if the original signal is much smaller or larger than this it will need to be amplified or attenuated to put it in the right range. Signals at so-called line level – such as the outputs from effects units, tape recorders, the analogue outputs of digital recorders and some electronic instruments – are already within this range, but the signal produced by a microphone may measure only a few thousandths of a volt.

To get the signal voltage up to a more manageable line level, any mixer designed for use with microphones will incorporate a special, low-noise microphone amplifier, right at the input, to bring the microphone signal up to the mixer's internal working level. This microphone pre-amplifier may also be fitted with phantom power circuitry, enabling it to be used with capacitor mic or DI boxes that require power to operate their onboard electronics.

Because not all microphones produce the same level of output, and because the output level depends on the proximity and loudness of the sound being recorded, the microphone amplifier is equipped with a gain control to determine the amount of amplification applied to the signal. Usually the mic channel will have a mic/line switch to determine whether the input needs to go through the mic amp or not, and there'll also be two different types of input connector: an XLR for the mic and a jack for the line. The simplest way to set the gain trim is to set the channel and output faders at their unity gain positions (the odB mark, about three quarters of the way up) and then feed in the loudest signal you're likely to encounter. Adjust the gain trim so the signal is just going into the red on the output meters and you're set. An alternative method is to use the console's PFL buttons, if present, so that the input gain trim can be set whilst watching the signal level on one of the main output meters.

Phantom Power

Capacitor microphones need an electrical voltage to polarise the capsule, while both capacitor and electret microphones use built-in pre-amplifiers, which also require electrical power. The majority of capacitor and back-electret mics are designed to work use phantom powering, though some back-electret models can also be run from batteries. Phantom powering gets its name because the supply current is fed along the hot and cold conductors of a balanced microphone cable and returned along the screen conductor. The standard phantom power supply voltage is 48V and is generated within the mixing console. It may be switched on globally or per channel, depending on the mixer, but only balanced microphones should be plugged into the mixer when the phantom power is active.

Mic Amps

On a typical mid-priced desk, the mic inputs will be on balanced XLR sockets and the line and tape inputs on quarter-inch jacks, which may or may not be balanced, though balanced jacks are preferable if your multitrack machine has balanced connectors. If you intend to use capacitor mics, phantom powering on the mic inputs should be considered essential as external phantom power supplies are relatively expensive. Note that tube microphones require their own special power supply due to the very high voltages needed to power the tubes. In theory it is quite safe (though pointless) to apply phantom power to a dynamic microphone, but only if it's wired for balanced operation – something you may be glad to know if your console has a global phantom power switch.

Because not all microphones produce the same level of output, and because the output level also depends on the proximity and loudness of the sound being recorded, the microphone amplifier is invariably equipped with a variable gain control. Line level signals also vary in amplitude to some extent, so the line input on a typical mixer will also be fitted with a gain control. On some professional mixers the microphone and line inputs will each have their own gain control, but on most home recording and semi-pro recording and mixing equipment a common control is used for both mic and line gain adjustment.

The Pad Switch

Yet another button you might come across at the top of the channel strip is the mic Pad switch. This is used to reduce the level of microphone signals on those occasions when the mic output is too high to be handled by the input amplifier. This situation rarely arises, but it could be encountered when a sensitive mic is placed near a loud sound source, such as a bass drum. The pad button generally cuts the input level down by 20dB (or by a factor of ten, thinking of it in terms of voltage) before the signal enters the input amplifier.

Your mixer may also have a Phase button, which inverts the phase of the mic input, or sometimes both the mic and line inputs. This is useful in multimic situations, where phase cancellation may be a problem. If you're using two mics directed towards the same sound source and aren't sure whether or not you have a problem, reverse the phase of one of the mics and see if the resulting sound is better or worse at the low-frequency end, at which most phase problems manifest themselves. As a rule, the position that gives the strongest level of bass is the one to use.

Mixer Basics

The fundamental job of any audio mixer is to combine two or more audio signals and to allow their levels to be independently adjusted. More refined designs include equalisation (essentially another term for tone controls), the provision to connect up external effects units or signal processors, and the ability to route signals and mixes of signals to different destinations. Why all of this should be so will become apparent shortly, but to start with I'll describe a basic four-channel mixer, capable of performing the simple task of mixing four signals into one. Because the mixer has only one output, the output signal in this case will be mono. For stereo output we'd need two signal paths: one to carry the left speaker signal and one to carry the right signal.

Figure 1.1 shows a simplified schematic of a four-channel mono mixer with simple bass and treble equalisation. Separate mic and line gain controls have been shown to aid clarity, but in practice a single, shared control is more likely. There are separate input sockets for both the microphone and line input signals, though again, on entry-level equipment such as some budget multitrackers, it is possible that a single socket will be used for both. A switch is commonly used to toggle between the microphone input and the line input when two separate sockets are provided – it is unusual to be able to use both mic and line inputs at the same time, though some designs do permit this.

Equalisation

Directly after the mic/line switch is the equalisation section, which can be as simple as the bass/treble (also known as the hi/lo) arrangement as shown here, but most mixers used in recording also have at least one mid-range control, which is often sweepable so that it can be 'tuned' to different frequencies.

basic Mixers

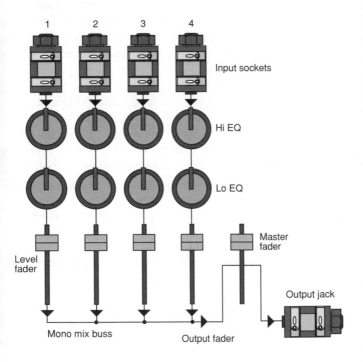

Figure 1.1: Simple four-channel mono mixer

Furthermore, all of the common types of EQ control offer cut as well as boost so that you can diminish some parts of the audio spectrum as well as accentuating them. Equalisation is a signal processing function, although it tends to be taken for granted because most mixers include it.

A refinement of the sweep control is found in the parametric equaliser, which allows you not only to tune into different frequencies but also to vary the range of frequencies it affects. This extra parameter is called bandwidth, or Q for short – the higher the Q the narrower the band of frequencies affected, and vice versa. Set to its highest Q an equaliser might be precise enough to affect a section of the audio spectrum less than a semitone wide, whereas a wide setting will affect several octaves. Because EQ can vary in both complexity and means of control, Chapter 3, 'Equalisers', is dedicated to explaining the subject in greater depth.

Before resorting to EQ you should endeavour to obtain the best possible sound at source. It cannot be stressed too highly that, if the sound is wrong to begin with, no amount of processing and EQ'ing will put it right; the old saying about 'fixing it in the mix' is pure myth when it comes to poor-quality sounds. The only exception to this is when you are using EQ to create a special effect rather than to restore tonal balance. What's more, unless used sparingly the EQ controls in low-cost mixing consoles can easily make a sound muddy or unnatural. Through using more sophisticated external equalisers it may be possible to make greater tonal changes without the sound becoming unnatural, but it's still good practice to use as little EQ as possible, especially in those cases where EQ boost is required.

If you have a very sophisticated desk it may well have other features in the EQ section. The frequencies at which the hi/lo control comes into effect might be switchable between two preset values, and there may also be a sub-bass filter you can switch in to attenuate any frequencies below the normal range of hearing. Sub-bass frequencies might be picked up from a resonant floor via a mic stand, or there may be traffic rumble that you need to keep out. Another advantage of using sub-bass cut is that, by stopping these unwanted frequencies from creeping into your recording system, you are preventing them from using up valuable headroom that could be better employed recording wanted signals at a higher level.

At the other end of the scale there may be a filter to cut out frequencies above the range of hearing. Such supersonic frequencies are often generated by electronic instruments and are best excluded, not only because they too use valuable headroom but also because they can 'beat' with other high frequencies to cause audible frequencies unrelated to the music. Most mixers have an additional switch which allows the equalisation section to be bypassed when not in use, and in general this is desirable as the less unnecessary circuitry you have in any signal path then the cleaner the signal will remain.

The Mix Buss

Finally, the signal level is controlled by a fader before it passes through a switch onto a piece of wire known as the *mix buss*, although on some simpler mixers the fader may be replaced by a conventional rotary control. There may also be a switch to isolate the output of an individual channel from the mix, and this will be labelled 'On' or 'Mute' depending on the manufacturer. Note that all four input channels are identical, and a larger mixer simply has more input channels.

Though the diagram shows the individual channels being connected directly to the mix buss, the circuitry involved is actually a little more complex. It is not necessary to understand the finer points of audio mixer design to be able to use one properly, though it is important to appreciate that, under normal circumstances, it is not possible to mix audio signals simply by connecting the outputs of several different pieces of equipment to a common piece of wire. To achieve mixing we need specialised mixing circuitry, which is one of the reasons we need to use a mixer.

The combined signal on the mix buss passes through a further stage of amplification known as a *mix amplifier*, in which the gain of the mix amplifier is controlled by the master level fader. The master level fader controls the output level of the mixer, allowing it to present the correct signal level to the amplifier or recorder fed by the mixer. The master fader may also be used to make controlled fades at the ends of each song.

Stereo Mixers

It requires only a few minor changes to turn a simple mono mixer into a stereo model, like the one shown in Figure 1.2. This mixer is in many ways similar to the one in Figure 1.1, with the exception that the input channels now have an extra control called pan. Pan is short for panorama, and is used to adjust the proportion of the channel signal being sent to each of the two busses. One buss is used to carry the left signal and the other carries the right, so that when the pan control is turned completely anti-clockwise the channel signal

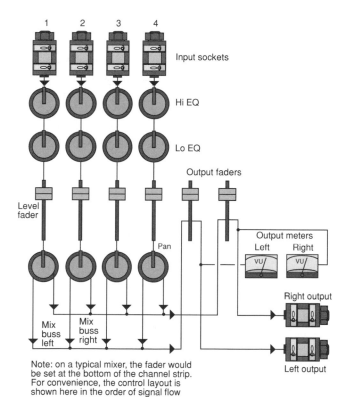

Note: on a typical mixer, the fader would be set at the bottom of the channel strip. For convenience, the control layout is shown here in the order of signal flow

Figure 1.2: Four-channel stereo mixer with meters

is routed exclusively to the left mix buss. Turning it clockwise routes the signal to the right buss, while setting it dead centre routes equal amounts of signal to the left and right busses. When reproduced over a stereo speaker system, the sound will move from the left to the right speaker as the pan control is turned from anticlockwise to clockwise. These two left and right busses are often referred to in the singular as a stereo mix buss, though in reality the two busses are still physically separate pieces of wire.

A stereo mixer has two master faders, one for the left signal and one for the right, though some mixers use a ganged control with a single knob or fader both to save on cost and space and to make using controlled fades easier. Figure 1.2 also shows a stereo level meter that allows the user to monitor the output level of the mixer. This type of meter will be familiar to anyone who has used a stereo cassette recorder, though the mechanism could also take the form of a moving-coil meter with a physical pointer, or it could be a row of LEDs (Light Emitting Diodes) arranged in the form of a ladder. Furthermore, the meter may read the RMS signal level (an averaged figure that corresponds closely with the perceived loudness of the sound), or it may be a peak programme type that follows the signal peaks more closely. As a rule, moving-coil meters read RMS levels, while LED, LCD, plasma and VDU displayed meters may be of either type.

Mixer Format

The simple stereo mixer illustrated so far is very commonly used in small PA (Public Address) systems, and its format is usually described in the form of something into two. A 12 into 2 (12:2) mixer, for example, has 12 input channels and two (left and right) outputs. The format becomes a little more involved when it comes to dedicated recording mixers, as you also have to include the number of output busses and the number of monitor channels. For example, a 32-channel in-line mixer with eight output groups, 32 monitor channels and a stereo output would be classified as a 32:8:32:2 mixer. These terms will be explained further throughout the course of this chapter.

Auxiliaries

Most recording mixers have an additional facility for connecting one or more external effects and also for producing an alternative cue or monitor mix for the performers. In a live situation the cue mix might be fed to the stage monitors or in-ear monitoring system, and may well have a different balance of instruments and voices to the main mix heard by the audience. In the studio this may be a musician's headphone mix.

This is necessary when, for example, the performance includes complex vocal harmonies and the singers need to hear more of the vocals than of the instrumental backing. Both adding effects and setting up the performer's cue monitoring can be handled using what are known as the mixer's *auxiliary controls*. Figure 1.3 explains how these work. Here you can see that two new controls have been added: Aux 1 and Aux 2, where *aux* is a shortened form of auxiliary.

Pre-Fade Send

Aux 1 is really just another level control, feeding a separate mono mix buss that runs across the mixer to the Aux 1 master level control and then to the Aux 1 output socket. The signal feeding the Aux 1 control is taken before the channel fader, and for this reason is known as a *pre-fade send*. The significance of a pre-fade send is that, once set, the level of the Aux 1 signal doesn't change if the channel fader setting is moved. It follows that a mono mix of all four channels can be set up using the Aux 1 controls, and this will appear at the Aux 1 master output, under the overall control of the Aux 1 master level control. This mix, being totally independent of the main fader settings, can provide the performers with a monitor mix that is exactly to their liking without compromising the main stereo mix.

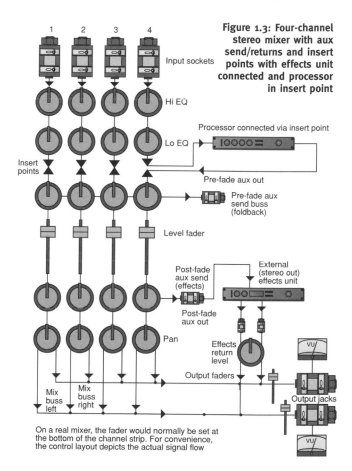

Figure 1.3: Four-channel stereo mixer with aux send/returns and insert points with effects unit connected and processor in insert point

On a real mixer, the fader would normally be set at the bottom of the channel strip. For convenience, the control layout depicts the actual signal flow

Post-Fade Send

The other aux control, Aux 2, is located after the channel fader (post-fader), and as a consequence its level is affected by changes in the channel fader's setting. This is exactly what's needed if Aux 2 is being used to feed an effect such as reverb, because when you use an effect connected via the aux send the unaffected or dry signal goes via the channel fader onto the stereo mix buss, and the effect unit output is then added to this later in the signal path.

As the channel fader setting is changed during the course of a mix, the amount of effect should generally change by exactly the same amount, thus maintaining the correct balance of effect to dry signal, and this can be achieved by using a post-fade aux send to drive the effects box. If we were to feed the effects from a pre-fade send, which is independent of the channel fader setting, the effect level would remain the same, regardless of the fader setting. For example, if you were to add reverb to a guitar in this way and then used the fader to bring the guitar level down to zero, the reverb would remain at a fixed level, even when the dry guitar had been faded to silence.

Why do we go to all of this trouble of devising an aux send system for connecting effects when we could simply pass the effected signal directly through an effects unit and into a mixer channel? The whole beauty of the aux send system is that, by using different settings of the post-fade Aux 2 control on each channel, it's possible to send different amounts of each channel's signal to the same effects unit. When the output from this effects unit is added to the main stereo mix, adjusting the Aux 2 controls on the individual channels allows different amounts of the same effect to be added to the various channel signals. A typical example might be where one reverberation unit is used to provide a rich reverb for the vocals, less reverb for the drums and little or none for the guitars and bass.

Wet And Dry Sounds

It is important to note that an effects unit used in conjunction with a channel aux send should generally be set up so that it produces only the effected sound and none of the original. This is usually accomplished by means of a mix control, which is either controlled by way of a physical knob or accessed via the effects unit's editing software. The effect-only sound is often known as the *wet* sound, so the mix should be set to 100% effect, 0% *dry*.

The output of the effect unit could simply be fed back into the mixer via any spare input channels, but you'll often find dedicated effects return inputs, also known as aux returns, provided for that purpose. Aux returns are electrically similar in nature to the mixer's input channels, but usually with far fewer facilities – they have no mic inputs, little or no EQ and few (if any) aux sends of their own. Normally, aux returns feed straight into the main stereo mix, although on some more elaborate consoles it may also be possible to feed them to other destinations.

If a spare input channel is used to feed an effect output into the mix, ensure that the corresponding aux send (in this case Aux 2) is turned down on the channel used as a return, or the effect signal will be fed back on itself, resulting in an unpleasant howl.

Stereo Effects

As the majority of effects units have stereo outputs, they need to be connected to either two spare input channels (usually panned hard left and right) or to a stereo aux return input. Figure 1.3 shows an external effects unit connected to the stereo aux return, where the two inputs feed the left and right stereo mix busses. It is sometimes possible to use just one of the effect outputs to feed into a single channel or return when mixer inputs are in short supply, but in this case the effect will be in mono only.

However, note that, although the controls shown in the figures are arranged in a logical order to illustrate the signal flow through the channel, commercial mixers tend to position the pan and aux controls above the channel fader, as the fader is the control which most often requires adjustment.

Insert Points

There is another standard way to connect an effects unit or signal processor to a mixer, and that is via an insert point. All but the most basic analogue mixers have insert points on their input channels and also on their master stereo outputs, though digital mixers may have more limited insert capabilities, mainly because of the additional cost of the necessary extra input and output converters. However, digital mixers and virtual mixing systems implemented on computers also tend to include both effects and signal processors that can be assigned to virtual insert points via the software interface.

An insert point is simply a means of breaking into a signal path at some point so that the signal can be diverted via the external effect or processor device. On most of the analogue mixers you are likely to encounter the insert points will be in the form of TRS (Tip, Ring, Sleeve) jack sockets, which means that you will need a specially wired Y-lead or adaptor to be able to use them. The TRS socket is conventionally wired tip send/ring return, but if soldering up leads is not your forte (though you'll save a lot of money if you learn) then you can buy an adaptor that will enable you to use off-the-shelf jack leads.

In Figure 1.3 the insert points are shown as black arrowheads, which show their position in the signal path – the sockets actually contain sprung contacts that maintain the signal flow when no plug is inserted. Physically, they appear as TRS jacks and are located with the other sockets, either along the top edge or rear panel of the mixer. It is very important to note that, while it is permissible to connect any type of effect or signal processor via an insert point, there are restrictions on what can be used via the aux send/return system.

Effects And Processors

This next section is very important, and understanding its implications will save you a lot of trouble and frustration when connecting effects and processors. In fact, it's so important that the information will occasionally be repeated throughout the book.

While it is permissible to connect any type of effect or signal processor via an insert point, there are restrictions on what can be used via the aux send/return system. As a rule of thumb, only delay-based effects such as reverb, echo, chorus, phasing, flanging and pitch shifting should be connected via the aux system, and these are generally called effects. If the box uses delay to do its work then it's an effect, and if there's a dry/effect mix knob or parameter then, again, the box is almost certain to be an effect. The unique quality of an effect is that it is added to the original signal. A process, such as EQ, doesn't add to the original signal but instead changes it. Processors include compressors, gates and EQ, and may normally only be connected via insert points, and not via the aux sends and returns. There are solutions to specific problems that may involve connecting processors to the aux send system, however, and these will be described later in this book.

Pre-Fade Listen

Most mixers include pre-fade listen (PFL) buttons that, when depressed, display the channel signal level on one of the desk's meters and isolate the channel in the monitor speakers or headphones. This facility provides an easy way of setting up levels independently of channel faders, and it also allows you to check individual signals in isolation. To set the input gain control of a mixer for the best signal-to-noise performance, it's simply a matter of going through the mix one channel at a time, pressing the PFL Solo button, and adjusting the input gain for a nominal full-scale reading on the output-level meter designated for PFL use. When you release the PFL button, all of the other channels will come back on and the meters will once again display the level of the output signal.

If there are no PFL buttons, the best way to optimise the channel gain is to set the channel fader at around three quarters of the way up, turn the stereo output faders to the 0dB positions, and then adjust the gain control to indicate a full-scale reading on the main output meters.

Some mixers also include a solo facility, which is again accessed via a button at the bottom of the channel strip. This function is similar to PFL in that it isolates the channel signal in the control room monitors, although both the signal level and pan position remain locked in place. With PFL, the signal is always monitored in mono and at a fixed level, regardless of the position of the fader. To solo a channel that has an effect applied, it is generally necessary to solo both the channel in question and the relevant effects return.

2 MULTITRACK MIXERS

As well as mixing signals, a studio console also acts as a central routing system, sending signals to the different tape machine tracks, adding effects from external processors and mixing the tape machine's outputs to produce a final stereo mix. At the same time it also has to function as a mixer within a mixer, so that a separate control-room monitor mix can be set up while the performers are recording or overdubbing their material. This makes it a lot more sophisticated than the four-into-two mixer mentioned earlier, and perhaps two of the most difficult areas to tackle are the multitrack outputs and the off-tape (or off-digital-recorder) monitoring.

Tracks Or Channels?

The terminology associated with mixers can be a little confusing, and a common mistake made by even experienced users is referring to a mixer as having so many 'tracks'. In fact mixers don't have any tracks: they have channels (inputs) and groups (outputs) – it's multitrack recorders that have the tracks!

So far we've described a simple input channel with input gain, EQ, aux sends, pan control and a fader, but on a multitrack mixer there are two different kinds of channel. The main input channel generally has the most comprehensive facilities, and is used to feed microphones and line-level sources into the mixer and subsequently to the recorder inputs while recording. When the recording is complete and you're mixing your recorded tracks, the input channels are free from the output from the multitrack recorder. The physical location of the monitor channels depends on whether you have a split or in-line mixer.

In order to hear what has already been recorded while adding new parts you will need monitor channels, which are used to set up a guide monitor mix based on the multitrack outputs. This is necessary as, without a monitor mix, there would be no way of keeping in tune or in time with pre-recorded material.

Monitor Channels

Monitor channels are similar to the main input channels, but on analogue consoles they often have fewer facilities and may have rotary level controls instead of faders. On an in-line mixer (so called because the main input and monitor controls are located in the same channel strip as those of the input channels) there's often a provision which enables you to switch all or part of the EQ between the main and monitor signal paths so that you can have your EQ where you most need it. The same is also often true of the aux sends. On digital consoles, it's more common to find both main and monitor channels with the same features. The main responsibility of the monitor channels during the recording phase of a project is in providing a rough mix of the recorded tracks to which the performers can play along.

It's generally easier to figure out the function of the monitor channels by envisaging the monitor section as a separate mixer in its own right, fed from the multitrack machine's outputs and routed into the main stereo mix.

There is no longer any need for a monitor mix once the recording has been completed, and this means that the monitor channels are available for other purposes. Most often they are used as extra line inputs at the mixing stage, during which they can function as either effects returns or additional input channels for sequenced MIDI instruments. At mixdown, the monitor channels invariably route into the main stereo mix.

Groups

For multitrack work, there must be some facility for sending different signals to different multitrack inputs, and this is where groups come into the picture. A stereo mixer just has a left and a right output, but a multitrack mixer needs several additional outputs to feed the individual tracks of the recording machine. Each of these outputs needs its own fader for setting recording levels. These separate outputs are collectively known as *groups*.

If you need to send a different signal or mix of signals to all eight inputs of an eight-track recorder you will need a mixer with eight group outputs in addition to the main stereo output. This is known as an *eight-buss console* because the eight groups are fed from eight separate mix busses. However, it isn't limited to eight-track recording – you can work with as many tracks as you like, as long as you don't need to record on more than eight tracks at any one time. This may involve a little repatching, but it's one way of getting a lot of performance from a relatively small mixer.

Routing Buttons

On the basic mixer channels can only be either on or off, but on a multitrack mixer they can also be routed to any of the groups, usually in odd/even pairs via the channel-routing switches. If two or more channels are routed to the same output they are automatically mixed together so that, if you wanted to, you could mix four tom mics and then route them all to channel five. The channel faders still set the relative levels of the various signals being mixed, but a master group fader controls the overall level being fed into the multitrack recorder.

Pan And Routing

In our original basic mixer, the pan control only steered the channel signal between the left and right outputs. In a multitrack console, however, it also steers the channel signal between the odd- and even-numbered busses of the buss pair to which that channel is routed. A single routing button handles the routing for a pair of groups. If it were necessary to route a channel to output group two, for example, you'd press the routing button marked 'one/two' and turn the pan control fully clockwise so that all of the signal went to group two and none to group one. Leaving the pan in its centre position would send equal amounts of signal to groups one and two. To record something in stereo (for example, the different tom mics on a drum kit), the relevant channels would be routed to a pair of groups and the pan control used to position the various sounds between them. The outputs from these two groups would then be recorded to two tracks of the multitrack recorder. When mixed, these tracks would be fed into separate mixer channels and then panned hard left and right in order to maintain the original stereo image.

Routing And Subgrouping

On an eight-buss mixer (the most common analogue mixer format used for project studio work) the routing buttons would be marked one to eight, with a further left/right button for routing the channel directly to the stereo mix. Figure 2.1 shows the path of the signal flow to the group fader and group output socket.

Just as the monitor channels change roles when switching from recording to mixing, so does the group routing system. During recording the groups are used to route signals to tape, but during the mix they can be routed back into the stereo mix. As always, there's a very good reason for this.

Imagine that you have a backing vocals section recorded over four or five tracks of your multitrack tape. In order to change the overall level of the backing vocals you'd have to move several faders at the same time, which is both cumbersome and inaccurate. A more effective approach is to create a subgroup of the backing vocals by routing the vocal channels to a pair of groups rather than directly to the left/right mix. In this way the whole stereo backing vocal mix can be controlled by using just two group faders. Some consoles have the groups permanently routed to the stereo mix, while other models provide groups-to-stereo buttons for each group fader,

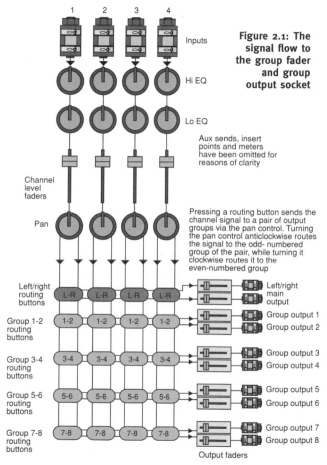

Figure 2.1: The signal flow to the group fader and group output socket

Inputs

Hi EQ

Lo EQ

Aux sends, insert points and meters have been omitted for reasons of clarity

Channel level faders

Pan

Pressing a routing button sends the channel signal to a pair of output groups via the pan control. Turning the pan control anticlockwise routes the signal to the odd-numbered group of the pair, while turning it clockwise routes it to the even-numbered group

Left/right routing buttons — L-R — Left/right main output

Group 1-2 routing buttons — 1-2 — Group output 1 / Group output 2

Group 3-4 routing buttons — 3-4 — Group output 3 / Group output 4

Group 5-6 routing buttons — 5-6 — Group output 5 / Group output 6

Group 7-8 routing buttons — 7-8 — Group output 7 / Group output 8

Output faders

and these generally route all odd-numbered group faders to the left and those that are even numbered to the right.

A better system, which is usually missing from budget consoles, is to provide group pan controls. With group pan controls you can create mono subgroups and still pan them anywhere in the stereo mix. If you don't have them you will always have to use two group faders for every subgrouping operation, apart from those where the end result will be panned either hard left or right.

In a typical mix you might create subgroups from drums, backing vocals and keyboards, which reduces the number of faders that need to be moved during the mix. Note, however, that any effects that are to be added to these subgroups using the aux sends should be returned to the same subgroup (using the channel or effect return routing buttons) or the effect level won't change when the group fader is moved. Figure 2.2 shows the signal flow at mixdown. Here the monitor channels are being used as extra line inputs, and the signal flow shows how subgroups actually work.

Split And In-Line Monitoring

Earlier in the chapter I mentioned in-line mixing consoles, and the concept is an important one as most modern consoles adopt the in-line format. On a

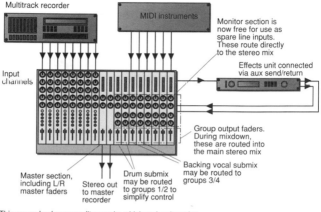

Multitrack recorder

MIDI instruments

Monitor section is now free for use as spare line inputs. These route directly to the stereo mix

Input channels

Effects unit connected via aux send/return

Group output faders. During mixdown, these are routed into the main stereo mix

Backing vocal submix may be routed to groups 3/4

Master section, including L/R master faders

Stereo out to master recorder

Drum submix may be routed to groups 1/2 to simplify control

This example shows a split console, which makes it easier to visualise the signal flow. However, the majority of project studio consoles follow the in-line format, in which the monitor controls are located within the channel strips

Figure 2.2: The signal flow at mixdown. The monitor channels are being used as extra line inputs and the signal flow shows how subgroups actually work

conventional split mixing console, the group faders and the monitor channel controls are situated on the right-hand side of the mixer and separated from the input channels by the master section. The master section includes functions such as the master stereo faders, the group faders and the aux send and return masters. You may also find a test oscillator, a talkback mic, mix/two-track monitor selection, headphone level control and other facilities.

A minimum of eight monitor channels are required to provide a monitor mix from an eight-track recorder, but many split consoles have 16 or more dedicated monitor channels for when it is necessary to work with more than 16 tracks. In-line consoles, on the other hand, have as many monitor channels as they have input channels. The basic requirements for a split console monitor channel are level and pan controls, though most also have some form of EQ and aux send controls. Figure 2.3 shows a multitrack split console with the monitor section moved away from the main body of the mixer to clarify signal flow, and the in-line monitor in Figure 2.4 exhibits similar facilities.

Multitrack Monitoring

Setting up the monitoring for multitrack work used to be a lot more complicated than it is today, but fortunately the majority of recorders now have an auto monitor mode, which means that it's always possible to monitor from the recorder's track outputs and still hear the required signal. If a track is being recorded you will hear the track input, but if the track is in playback mode then you will automatically hear the recorded track. When executing a punch-in, the monitoring

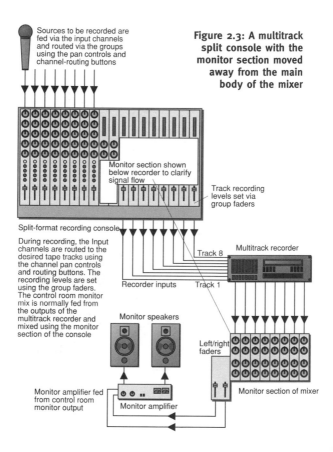

Sources to be recorded are fed via the input channels and routed via the groups using the pan controls and channel-routing buttons

Figure 2.3: A multitrack split console with the monitor section moved away from the main body of the mixer

Monitor section shown below recorder to clarify signal flow

Track recording levels set via group faders

Split-format recording console

During recording, the Input channels are routed to the desired tape tracks using the channel pan controls and routing buttons. The recording levels are set using the group faders. The control room monitor mix is normally fed from the outputs of the multitrack recorder and mixed using the monitor section of the console

Track 8

Multitrack recorder

Recorder inputs   Track 1

Monitor speakers

Left/right faders

Monitor section of mixer

Monitor amplifier fed from control room monitor output

Monitor amplifier

45

basic Mixers

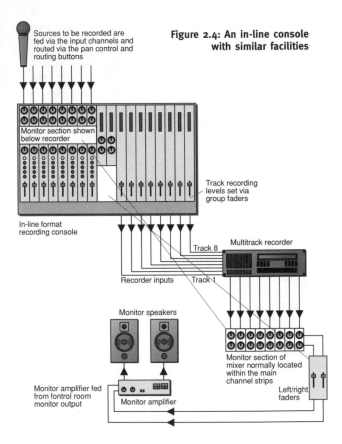

Figure 2.4: An in-line console with similar facilities

Sources to be recorded are fed via the input channels and routed via the pan control and routing buttons

Monitor section shown below recorder

In-line format recording console

Track recording levels set via group faders

Multitrack recorder

Track 8

Recorder inputs   Track 1

Monitor speakers

Monitor section of mixer normally located within the main channel strips

Left/right faders

Monitor amplifier fed from fontrol room monitor output

Monitor amplifier

automatically changes from track to input and then back to track again as you punch out. Usually, once the recorder is stopped the input signal is monitored.

More On In-Line Consoles

Virtually all budget recording consoles follow the in-line format, and the layout may seem confusing at first because the monitor and input controls are set in the same channel strip. There are advantages, however, not least being that, instead of being limited to just eight or 16 monitor channels, there is one monitor channel for every input channel. This arrangement usually results in a mixer that is physically deeper, from front to back, than an equivalent split design, but it also it means the mixer can be made narrower and still have the same number of channels.

Rather than reconfigure the whole mixer after recording to make it ready for mixing, most in-line consoles have a channel-flip switch that routes the track signal through the input channel and connects the unused monitor channel input to the channel-input sockets. The input channel fader may be used for balancing the mix if channels are flipped as soon as they have been recorded so that, by the time the recording is complete, the mix will already be set up on the input channel faders.

Split EQ And Aux Sends

Split consoles may or may not have EQ on the monitor channels, though they will usually have some aux sends. On an in-line desk, however, both aux sends and EQ facilities may have to be shared. The monitor sections of most split consoles have at least one dedicated aux send control so that effects may be added to the foldback or cue mix, but there may be little or no room to include EQ or any further aux send controls.

To get around this, there's usually a switching arrangement that allows the monitor channel to share part of the main input channel's EQ. For example, if the main EQ is a four-band affair with two sweep mids then the monitor channel may be able to make use of the hi and lo EQ, thus leaving the main input channel with two sweeps. In such cases the sweep range is usually wide enough to allow the two mids to cover the entire audio spectrum.

Another common arrangement is to have a setup whereby a couple of the aux sends are switchable between either the input or monitor channels. This is obviously less than ideal, but providing a full-featured EQ on every monitor and input channel would take up a lot of space and add considerably to the cost of the desk.

Monitors As Line-ins

When you're mixing down using an in-line console the channel flip switches are all operated, leaving the monitor channels connected to the console's line inputs and available to accommodate other line signals that may need to be added to the mix. If you have a large MIDI system synchronised to a multitrack recorder then these additional inputs may well prove necessary, unless you have the luxury of a separate keyboard mixer. However, these spare monitor channels may also be used to handle extra effects returns if you run out of the conventional varieties (remember that an effects return is just another kind of line-level input channel).

All-Input Mixing

No overview of mixers would be complete without looking at the 'all-input' method of working, which can be applied to both split and in-line consoles. In all-input mode, the monitor channels are not once used for monitoring. This may sound completely illogical, but it's actually a very simple way of working.

If you have an eight-track recorder and enough mixer input channels to play with you can leave the outputs of your recorder permanently connected to the first eight input channels of the mixer, routing these directly to the stereo left/right mix so that you can monitor them. You can then use the remaining input channels to handle the signals being recorded, routed via the groups. This removes the need to toggle the off-tape signals between the monitor and input channels, so that you can leave your MIDI equipment permanently connected to the monitor inputs. Using this method, your control-room mix becomes your final mix. In fact I think that this is the simplest way to work, provided of course that you have at least eight more input channels than you have recorder tracks.

The only limitation of working this way (other than having to ensure you have a mixer with enough input channels) is that the monitor channels can't be routed via the groups to create subgroups – they always feed directly into the stereo L/R mix. However, as most MIDI sequencers allow you to automate synth and sampler levels and pans via MIDI, being unable to group MIDI instrument inputs shouldn't be a disadvantage.

Monitor Selecting

The control room monitor outputs of a console normally follow the stereo mix present on the master faders, but sometimes you'll want to hear playback from one or more stereo-mastering machines or the output from an effects processor, or you may need to check what is being fed out of one of your aux send sockets. A row

124549

of buttons in the master section provides a choice of monitoring options, though not all consoles provide the same choices. Pressing a PFL or solo button overrides the stereo mix so that you only hear the soloed channel on the control room monitors or headphones, but this doesn't interfere with the stereo output.

The monitor output also has its own master volume control, and it often a dim switch as well. Dim is a useful function: basically, it drops the monitor volume to about ten per cent at the touch of a button so that you can make yourself heard in the studio or answer phone calls without having to resort to manually alter the setting on the volume control. On the majority of budget desks the headphone outputs are fed from the same source as the monitor output, although the headphones are usually fitted with a separate volume control.

Talkback

Talkback is necessary for the engineer to be able to speak to the musicians in the studio area. Often there is a talkback mic built into the mixer itself, but on some desks there will be an XLR socket on the front panel fashioned to accept a gooseneck-style mic. The mic is normally routed into the musician's foldback system (a headphone amplifier or a small pair of monitor speakers), though it's also common to have the option of routing it to tape so that you can record cues or song titles as you go along. Talkback switches work only when depressed, to stop you from leaving them on accidentally. In the studio, talkback overrides whatever else is being fed to the studio monitor system but doesn't affect the control room monitor system. And, of course, effects are not used with talkback.

Automation

Console-level automation is now relatively affordable in analogue consoles, often as a VCA-driven add-on, though the most basic form of automation is simple channel muting, which may be controlled by means of a MIDI sequencer. Though this might seem very basic, it can offer possibilities other than simply shutting down channels when not in use in order to minimise noise. For example, a signal could be split and fed to two channels simultaneously, with the mutes being used to select between them. In this way a track shared between lead vocals and guitar solo, for example, could be mixed by pre-setting the appropriate effect and EQ treatments for guitar and vocals on each of the two channels and then switching between them automatically at the right moment. Level changes could be performed in the same way (ie switching between two channels on which all of the settings, except level, are identical).

Digital Mixers

Digital consoles don't have the same space restrictions as analogue mixers, and many of the controls are accessed one at a time by means of a data-entry knob or a single row of faders, which can be switched to control all of the channel levels, all of the aux send levels, all of the group output levels and so on. Having four bands of fully parametric EQ on both the monitor and input channels is not uncommon, and you may find the same facilities on the main buss outputs and effects returns.

Digital mixers perform essentially the same function as their analogue counterparts, the main practical difference being the user interface. Because of the prohibitive cost of using converters to provide a counterpart of every physical aux send, return and insert point on a typical analogue desk, most digital mixers provide a number of on-board effects and processors to circumvent this limitation. There may also be a digital link between the mixer and compatible digital multitrack machines, or computer-based systems using the same I/O protocol, such as the ADAT optical interface, which preserves signal integrity and makes wiring the thing up easier.

Because digital mixers can incorporate more features

than analogue consoles, it would be impractical to provide a physical control for each function. Instead there is usually a physical fader for each channel (which are generally motorised on an automated mixer) but only one set of EQ and aux send controls, or even just a single data knob. A selector button by the side of each fader allows the control section to become active for that particular channel, and a display screen usually provides further information as well as a physical representation of some of the virtual controls.

Because most digital consoles include effects, dynamic processing and the ability to automate complete mixes, right down to EQ and aux settings, it is possible to recall an old mix many months later and get it back exactly as it was. Having to rely on the on-board processors (due to the lack of insert points on every channel and buss) is a mixed blessing, as you may feel that you could get better results from using an external processor, but you have no way of connecting it to the system. It may therefore be more convenient for you to feed the digital multitrack back into the mixer via its analogue channel inputs so that analogue effects and processors can be inserted between them when required during the mixing process. This is most easily achieved if the recorder is connected to the mixer via a patchbay.

Digital Advantages

It's arguable whether digital mixers have any sonic advantage over analogue consoles – they're certainly less straightforward to use. However, they do make it possible to access and automate a great number of functions at a relatively low cost and in a very compact form. Furthermore, we've now reached the stage where it's often cheaper for a manufacturer to build a completely automated digital mixer than an equivalent manually operated analogue mixer.

A simple digital mixer will normally offer at least snapshot or scene-automation facilities, whereby the whole setup of the console can be stored and recalled at the touch of a button. Such scene memories are particularly useful in live sound situations, in which a different scene can be saved for each song or for each band using the mixer.

Some of the more sophisticated designs of mixer provide full dynamic automation, which means that gradual control changes can be recorded as well as sudden changes. Depending on the mixer, the automation may be fully self-contained, or it may rely on an external desktop Macintosh or PC. The input of some form of timecode from the recorder is required to keep the mixer automation synchronised with the recording – MTC (MIDI Time Code) or SMPTE timecode are the most commonly used systems.

One great advantage of using a digital mixer with a digital multitrack recorder is that the signal may be kept in the digital domain by using a digital interface, such as the ADAT optical protocol. Indeed, if you use a digital master recorder, such as a DAT machine, the signal may never need to leave the digital domain again until it reaches the listener's hi-fi system. As a rule, the most significant signal deterioration occurs whenever analogue signals are converted to digital signals or vice versa, so once a signal is in the digital domain it makes sense to keep it there.

Digital Inputs

With an analogue mixer you can combine inputs from as many different sources as you like, but with a digital mixer things aren't quite that simple when you want to combine a number of digital inputs. This is because all components of a digital system must be running at the same sample rate, and they must be synchronised so that errors aren't passed from one device to another with the data. If you're feeding a digital multitrack machine into a digital mixer via an ADAT link or similar interface it's usual for the multitrack machine to generate the master clock and for the mixer to 'slave' to this clock.

However, if you were to try to plug in a CD player or a DAT recorder to another digital input on the mixer, it wouldn't be in sync with the multitrack and you'd either hear a distorted mess or, at best, occasional loud clicks. A similar problem occurs if you have one digital source running at 44.1kHz and another at 48kHz.

In professional studios this is remedied by using a single 'house clock' to provide a word-clock feed, which is then connected to all of the digital machines in the studio, forcing them all to run in sync (though they must all be capable of running at the same sample rate for this to work). However, many semi-pro devices don't have a word-clock input, so this tidy solution can't always be implemented. One solution is for mixer manufacturers to provide one or more digital inputs fitted with ASRCs (Asynchronous Sample Rate Converters). These inputs take any digital sample rate, synchronised or not, and then convert it to the correct sample rate, synchronised to the internal workings of the mixer. In theory a small degradation in signal quality occurs when an ASRC is used, but in most cases it is negligible.

When no ASRC input is available and word-clock sync is not possible, the only alternative is to run the analogue output of the external device to one of the analogue inputs of the console. Again, this will result in a slight loss of quality, and level matching will be necessary, but the subjective difference should be very small.

Specifications

The mixer is the centre of your studio and all signals pass through it at some point. Because of this it must have the highest possible electrical performance in terms of frequency response, distortion and noise. On budget mixing consoles the mic input amplifiers are often the weak link in terms of noise, and you'll find that, as you turn up the mic gain control, the background noise increases along with it. This is further compounded by the tendency of budget studios to make extensive use of dynamic or moving-coil microphones because of their versatility and cheapness. Unfortunately, their low sensitivity means that a great deal of gain is needed to record quiet instruments such as the acoustic guitar or shy vocalists, and so noise becomes a real problem. The only practical way to avoid this is to buy at least one good-quality condenser or back-electret microphone for use in difficult recording situations, as these have a much higher output than dynamic mics.

The quality of the signal will also be compromised if any other pieces of equipment are connected to the mixer – like any other chain, an audio chain is only as strong as its weakest link, so you should really only buy effects and processors that have good noise and distortion specifications.

Effects And Processors

When connecting signal processors to mixing consoles, it is best to consider the processors as falling into two distinct categories, each of which must be handled differently: those which treat the whole signal and those which add a proportion of treated signal to the unprocessed signal in order to create their effect. Even though both types are strictly speaking processors of some kind, I have used the term processor here to describe those devices that treat the whole signal and the term effect for those where a mix of processed and unprocessed sound is involved. Fortunately, there is a general rule that may be applied to decide which is which. If the device includes some kind of time-delay circuit then it is almost certainly an effect – if it does not then it is a processor.

Some examples of processors include gates, expanders, compressors, limiters, equalisers, enhancers and distortion devices, all of which are can be characterised by having no mix control (with the exception of enhancers, on which the mix control determines the depth of the effect). Some examples of effects include reverberators, digital delay lines, chorus units, flangers, ADT units and pitch shifters, all of which usually have a mix facility, thus enabling the user to blend the processed and unprocessed sound together within the unit. However, by setting the mix control to output the effected signal only, mixing can be (and generally is) performed within the mixing console.

An effect may be used either in conjunction with the auxiliary send circuit (in which case any mixing is performed by the mixer itself) or via an insert point (in which case the unit's own mix control is used). A processor, on the other hand, is normally used only at the insert point, or otherwise connected in line with the signal path. Any attempt to use it via the aux send system is likely to yield unpredictable and undesirable results. At best the resulting sound will be diluted by the addition of the untreated portion of the signal, and in the worst case phase differences within the circuitry may completely spoil the tonality of the signal.

An exception to this rule occurs when you need to treat one channel with a signal processor, such as a compressor, but you don't have an insert point available. In this case, you can feed the compressor from the pre-fade aux send and turn the channel fader down completely. The compressor output may then be plugged into a spare channel. The compression would normally only be added to a single channel, so all of the corresponding pre-fade sends on the other channels should also be turned down completely. However, if you want to compress a mix of similar sounds, such as backing vocals, then you could feed all of these to the pre-fade send buss and compress them as a single mixed signal.

If it proves necessary to split a signal in order to feed two inputs, a simple Y-lead or two-into-one adaptor will usually do the job. However, the same is unfortunately not true when two outputs are required to feed one input. If two outputs are joined directly there is a likelihood that distortion or even circuit damage might result, so the only valid way to combine two signals is via a proper mixer circuit designed for the purpose.

However, it's important that you should under no circumstances attempt to connect the speaker output of an amplifier directly to any input of a mixing console or signal processor. If it proves necessary to extract a manageable signal from a speaker output, as may be the case when direct injecting a guitar or bass in order to preserve the sound of the amplifier, then a purpose-made DI box must be used to match the signal levels.

Effects Connections

The usual way to connect a reverb unit or other effect is to feed it from a post-fade effects send on the console (effectively mono) and then feed the two reverb outputs back into the mixer, either through two effects returns panned left and right or through a pair of spare input channels. The effects unit output mix parameter or control is then set for effect only – no dry signal. If you use input channels as returns, it is important to ensure that the corresponding aux send is turned off completely on those channels or some of the reverb will be fed back to its own input, causing feedback or tonal coloration.

To make sure that your reverb unit or multi-effects processor works as quietly as possible, set the aux sends on the channels you want to effect to around three quarters up. The aux send master should also be set to three quarters up – the input level control on the effects unit itself is used to determine the signal level going into the unit so that a healthy meter reading is obtained. You should set the output level of the effects unit to be close to maximum and then adjust the effects return level on the mixer to give you the right subjective level of effect. By following this procedure you will have ensured that the gain structure of both your mixer and your effects unit have been properly optimised.

It's also important to turn down any effects sends and to deactivate any mixer channels that aren't being used in the mixing process. This doesn't just mean turning the fader down; it's also necessary to turn the channel off completely if it has a mute button, and if you're using a console with routing buttons then you must make sure that any unused channels aren't routed to the main stereo mix. People don't often realise that a muted channel with the fader turned down can still add a little noise (known as *mix-buss noise*) just by being connected to the stereo mix buss, so it's always a good idea to unroute those channels not currently in use.

Mix-buss noise also applies to effects-send controls, but few consoles allow you to mute these. However, your desk may have aux send switching, which, for example, will allow you to route a channel's aux sends to either sends one and two or three and four. If this is indeed the case, and you only need to use two effects units in your mix, then use sends one and two for your effects, and on any channels on which effects aren't required route to sends three and four instead. This has the overall effect of removing any unused sends from the aux mix buss, which can make things considerably quieter.

Finally, if you're adding a specific effect to only one channel then you could take your effects send from the channel's insert send or from the channel's direct output, if it has one. Doing this should remove the addition of mix buss noise altogether. Alternatively, you could feed the signal to be treated directly into the effects unit itself and then feed the effects unit outputs into two adjacent mixer channels panned hard left and hard right. The effect/mix balance will then have to be set on the effects unit. It should also be realised, however, that a mono-in/stereo-out effects device, such as a digital reverb unit, will need to be fed into two mixer channels panned left and right if the stereo effect is to be preserved.

Processors are generally connected via a channel or group insert points on a console, though both effects and processors can be connected directly in line between a line-level signal source and a mixer input if you prefer. However, it is important in this case to realise that most outboard equipment only works properly with line-level inputs, and not with microphone signals. The only exception to this rule applies to equipment that includes a microphone pre-amplifier, such as dedicated voice channels or vocal processors.

Live Sound Consoles

Live mixers are very similar to studio mixers, with the exception that they have no need for multitrack return inputs. However, a live event may require a more complex monitor or foldback system than that used in a studio recording situation, which is why some of the larger stage consoles have something called matrix outputs. Figure 2.5 should clarify this potentially confusing subject.

Essentially, the matrix system employs several rows of knobs that allow the user to set up several different mono mixes based on the group signals (busses one to eight in an eight-buss desk), the main left/right signals and possibly signals from an external source. The buss signals will usually be picked up before they reach the fader so that the matrix mix is unaffected by adjustments to the group or master faders. Some mixers also have a mono master output in addition to the stereo outputs, and this may also be available on the matrix. In addition to the individual level knobs each row of the matrix will have a master level control, and probably mute and solo buttons as well. The mixes created using the matrix may be used to feed dressing-room or foyer mixes in a theatre, multitrack recorder inputs for live recordings, or even delay towers in a large concert system.

To investigate delay towers in depth wold be to exceed the scope of this book, but essentially they are separate PA speaker systems arranged at a distance from the stage and pointing towards the rear of the audience. Because sound travels at just over one foot per

basic Mixers

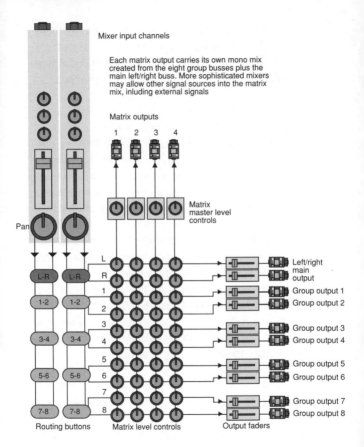

Mixer input channels

Each matrix output carries its own mono mix created from the eight group busses plus the main left/right buss. More sophisticated mixers may allow other signal sources into the matrix mix, inluding external signals

Matrix outputs

1 2 3 4

Matrix master level controls

Pan

L — Left/right main output
R

1 — Group output 1
2 — Group output 2

3 — Group output 3
4 — Group output 4

5 — Group output 5
6 — Group output 6

7 — Group output 7
8 — Group output 8

Routing buttons   Matrix level controls   Output faders

Figure 2.5: The matrix system

66

millisecond these remote speakers must be fed with a delayed signal so that the people near them hear the sound at the same time as the people near the main speakers at the front. Delay towers are often used at outdoor festivals, where audiences may be very large.

Test Oscillators

A test oscillator generates a steady mid-range tone, usually at 400Hz, which may then be sent to the main output busses to help calibrate levels or trace breaks in the signal chain. There may be a choice of different frequencies which can be selected, and the oscillator will also be fitted with an on/off switch and a level control. The way in which the oscillator is routed to the different mixer outputs varies between one mixer and another, but it's usually fairly self-explanatory.

Pink Noise

Because the majority of venues are acoustically imperfect, it's often necessary to equalise the PA feed in order to compensate for the worst of the room resonances. This is often achieved by feeding pink noise – a random signal with an equal amount of energy per octave – into the speaker system and then checking the frequency response shape by using a spectrum analyser. A graphic equaliser can then be set up to 'notch out' any serious room resonances. Several of the larger live mixing consoles have a pink noise generator built in for this purpose, and these tend to be located near the test oscillator.

Stage Talkback

Talkback is method by which the engineer can plug a mic into the mixer via a special talkback mic input and communicate with other members of the crew or the band via the mixer's various outputs. For example, the engineer could talk into the stage wedge monitor mix via the aux sends to communicate with the band, or there may be an external talkback output enabling the signal to be run to a monitor engineer operating a separate console by the side of the stage. On a typical mid-sized PA console, the talkback will be routable to the various aux outputs, the matrix section and an external talkback out socket. In most instances, a mic on a flexible gooseneck stand is plugged directly into the talkback mic XLR, and the talkback is operated by a non-latching button so that you don't get caught out by leaving it on while you're insulting the drummer!

Multicores

Unless the mixer is on stage with you for self-operation, you are likely to need a multicore to feed the mic signals from the stage to the console. A multicore is simply a bunch of small-diameter mic cables inside a common protective outer sheath, and it is important that you use the type containing individually screened pairs rather than the type which provides only a single outer screen for all of the cables. At the stage end, the multicore (or snake, as it is sometimes known) terminates in a metal box, upon which XLR sockets are mounted. A good strain-relief system is necessary to alleviate stress on the cable ends and soldered joints when the cable is packed and unpacked. There will be a limit to the cable's flexibility, so always follow the manufacturer's recommendations regarding minimum winding diameter when stowing the cable or winding it onto a drum.

At the mixer end a small multicore may simply terminate in a bunch of flying jack leads, but for larger systems it's common practice to fit a multi-pin connector to the end of the cable and fix the mating half of the connector onto the flight case bottom of the mixer. In this case, the mixer would be permanently fixed to the flight case bottom and a series of short cables used to connect the mixer inputs to the multi-pin connector. This greatly simplifies the setting-up procedure, as the individual mixer input connections need never be disturbed – all you need to do is connect one large multi-pin connector.

Depending on the complexity of the system, a separate cable or multicore is recommended to take the mixer's main and foldback outputs back to the stage for connection to the power amplifiers. Power amplifiers should always be set up as close to the speakers as possible in order to minimise the length of speaker cable used, which means that quite long signal cables may be required.

3 EQUALISERS

Chapter 1 touched on the basics of equalisation as it applies to mixing consoles, but the subject is important enough to be worthy of explanation in greater depth. The term equaliser was originally coined to describe a filter used to compensate for imperfections in the microphone signal chain, but in the context of recording and live mixing equalisation (or EQ, for short) is really just another term for tone control. While early studio equipment – and, to a greater extent, the analogue telephone lines for which EQ was first developed – need a lot of corrective EQ to make them sound natural, modern recording equipment is capable of storing and reproducing sound that is virtually identical to the original. Nevertheless, the original sound isn't always what we want to hear, so EQ has evolved to take on more of a creative role.

Equalisers are based around electronic circuits known as *filters*. Strictly speaking a filter is a device that removes something, but in the context of the circuits of active equalisers filters can be arranged within special circuit configurations so that they can boost as well as cut.

Early equalisers were very simple affairs, usually comprising no more than a single tone control offering only varying degrees of treble or bass cut. The first serious active equaliser to find popular acceptance was designed by the British electronic engineer Peter J Baxandall and comprised separate bass and treble controls, both of which could provide either cut or boost. This meant that the controls had to be set to their centre positions if the signal was to pass through unaffected.

What EQ Does

How does an equaliser work? It's helpful in this case to think of the operation of ordinary gain or volume controls, which turn the whole signal up or down in level without affecting the tonal balance. All of the frequencies present in the input signal are increased or decreased by the same amount, so that the sound which comes out is exactly the same as the signal that went in, in every aspect apart from level. A circuit that changes nothing but the level of a signal is said to have a flat frequency response. It is technically impossible to make a circuit that has an infinitely wide frequency response, but in the context of audio a circuit that is flat between the upper and lower limits of human hearing (generally between 20Hz and 20kHz) is said to have a flat response.

Unlike level or gain controls, the equaliser is designed specifically to affect the level of some frequencies more than others. A typical treble control, for example, raises or lowers the level of the high frequencies while leaving the low-frequency level virtually unchanged. The reason I say virtually is that, if you were to plot out the gain-versus-frequency characteristics of an equaliser on a graph, you'd find that the graph followed a curve – you don't see a sudden step at the frequency where the equaliser is set to operate. Cutting or boosting frequencies above 5kHz by so many decibels doesn't simply leave frequencies below that point unaffected (the effect is progressive) but also, the further below 5kHz you go, the less those frequencies are affected. This is much easier to understand if you take a look at Figure 3.1.

Figure 3.1 shows the bass-cut curves of a Baxandall-type equaliser in graphic form. Notice that the cut and boost curves eventually flatten out rather than rising indefinitely. This particular equaliser characteristic is described as a shelving response, because the cut or boost part of the curve eventually forms a flat shelf. It is possible to make an equaliser with a degree of

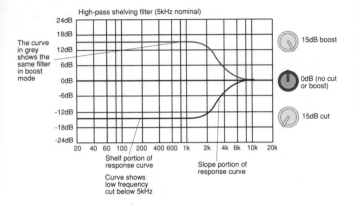

Figure 3.1: Shelving equaliser

boost which continues to increase with frequency, but this is usually undesirable. In the case of treble control, for example, it would mean that the higher the frequency, the more boost you'd have, and so much more boost than necessary would be applied at very high and even supersonic frequencies. This would lead to an increase in high-frequency noise and the possibility of the circuitry being overloaded to the point of distortion by frequencies too high even to hear. Conversely, a bass equaliser with similar characteristics would give proportionally more boost with a reduction in frequency, and so would give rise to problems with rumbling and humming, which can also overload electronics very easily. This is why most equalisers used in studio work tend to be either shelving or bandpass equalisers, both of which will be discussed later on in this book.

The filter slope of an equaliser is usually specified in decibels per octave, and for music applications slopes of 6dB and 12dB per octave are common. The greater the number of decibels per octave the sharper the filter slope, and frequencies outside the band are affected to a lesser degree. If it is required to filter out subsonic

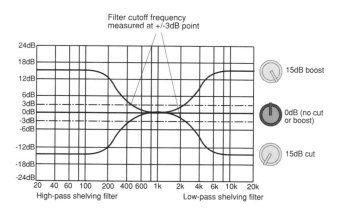

Figure 3.2: Low- and high-pass filters

signals (say, below 50Hz) or very high frequencies (above 20kHz or so) using a cut filter then even sharper slopes of 24dB per octave are used and the filters are non-shelving varieties. Such filters are described as high-pass and low-pass filters, because they allow high and low frequencies respectively to be passed through, and are often found on more comprehensive mixing consoles, microphone pre-amplifiers and sometimes on stand-alone equalisers. Figure 3.2 shows typical response curves for such filters.

Bandpass Filters

Shelving filters either cut or boost the levels of signals above or below a certain value. However, there's another kind of filter, known as a *bandpass* or *bell-curve equaliser*, which is commonly used in mid-range controls. This device confines its activities to a specific band of frequencies, leaving those above or below its range essentially unaffected. Figure 3.3 shows the characteristics of a typical bandpass filter in both cut and boost positions. The range of frequencies affected is a function of the EQ circuit design, and it's apparent that the wider the band of frequencies affected then the wider the response curve will be. The filter's bandwidth, or range, is defined by the width of the curve at the two points where the level is 3dB below the peak level. This is marked on Figure 3.3.

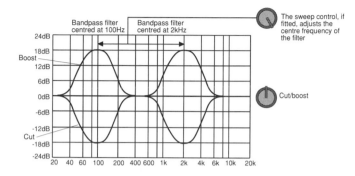

Figure 3.3: Bandpass filter

If you divide the centre frequency of the curve by its bandwidth, you get a figure known as the *Q* of the equaliser. This is a useful figure, because the larger the Q, the sharper the filter. High Q values are useful for picking out sounds that occupy a very narrow part of the audio spectrum, while lower Qs produce a smoother, more musical sound. In practice, it's possible to build high-Q analogue filters that affect a range of frequencies narrower than one semitone, and digital filters can be designed to affect a much narrower range than this.

Because of their ability to affect only a specific band of frequencies, bandpass equalisers are often chosen for use as mid controls, when one or more may be used. In a simple equaliser the bandwidth and centre frequency would be fixed, and the only option available to the user would be to vary the amount of cut or boost. However, most professional recording mixers have what are known as *sweep equalisers*, on which the Q is still fixed but the centre frequency of the equaliser can be adjusted.

Some console manufacturers also make it possible to switch the bass and treble (hi/lo) controls from a shelving to a bell or bandpass response, which makes the equaliser more flexible. A bell response might be useful when trying to add punch to a bass drum sound. Most bass drums have a 'note' at around 80–90Hz, so using an 80Hz bell equaliser allows the bass drum to be brought up to that level without unduly increasing the level of other unwanted sounds occurring below this frequency. A shelving equaliser, on the other hand, would increase the level of anything below 80Hz by the same amount. In musical terms, using the bell equaliser might produce a noticeably tighter sound than would be obtained through using a shelving equaliser and would boost the whole bass end in an indiscriminate way.

It's usual for the maximum cut or boost of equalisers used in recording to be limited to somewhere around 15dB, although some designs offer up to 18dB. Adding more than this may increase the signal level at the filter's frequency so much that it exceeds the available headroom (the circuit's safety margin), resulting in distortion.

Parametric EQ

If a third control is added to provide a continually variable Q then the sweep equaliser becomes a fully parametric equaliser. Here all of the important parameters are placed under the user's control: the degree of cut or boost, the frequency at which the cut or boost is centred and the width of the audio spectrum

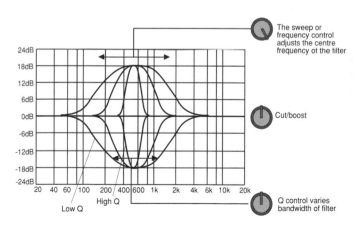

Figure 3.4: Parametric equaliser

affected. An outboard parametric equaliser usually comprises at least two filter sections, and often four, so as to provide independent control in different parts of the audio spectrum. Because there are three controls for each band setting up a parametric equaliser effectively takes time and experience, and those models that have individual bypass buttons for each individual band are easier to set up than models that have just a single bypass button for the whole unit. The response of a parametric equaliser is shown in Figure 3.4.

Graphic Equalisers

It's possible to exert a good degree of control over the entire audio spectrum by putting several narrow, fixed-frequency bell equalisers together in one box, all operating at different frequencies, and this is the basic operating idea of the graphic equaliser. Either constant Q or constant bandwidth filters may be used, and there's some argument over which sounds the best. A constant Q filter, as the name suggests, has the same Q value regardless of the degree of cut or boost applied, which means that the bandwidth of the filter actually changes. With a constant bandwidth filter it's the Q value that changes in order to achieve a constant bandwidth.

The individual filters are most often placed at either octave, half-octave or third-octave intervals and are arranged to overlap in such a way that, when they are all set to cut or boost by the same amount, the frequency response remains essentially flat. The sliders often have a centre detent so that this position can be readily identified. It's also common to find that the very highest and lowest frequency sliders control a shelving filter rather than a bell filter. Figure 3.5 shows the responses of the filters in a typical graphic equaliser. Again, the filter range is usually limited to a maximum of plus or minus 15dB.

The name *graphic equaliser* is derived from the fact that, because the equaliser is fitted with slider controls

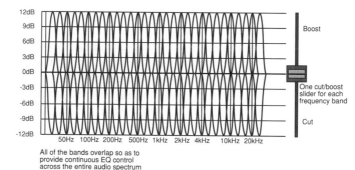

All of the bands overlap so as to
provide continuous EQ control
across the entire audio spectrum

Figure 3.5: Graphic equaliser

rather than rotary ones, the sliders provide a graphic representation of the frequency response of the equaliser. Graphic equalisers are reasonably flexible and easy to set up, but in practice they're better suited to live sound applications than to studio work, where their fixed-frequency filters make them less precise than a parametric equaliser. Furthermore, less sophisticated designs may adversely affect the sound of the signal being processed, and it's common for adjacent bands to interact in such a way that the actual EQ curve doesn't quite match the curve shown by the sliders. It's quite common to find graphic equalisers built into the master sections of live sound mixers, though they tend to have fewer bands than serious outboard units.

Desk Channel EQ

A typical mixing console has both high and low shelving controls set at around 100Hz and 10kHz, with two sweep mids covering the range in between. There's usually some overlap between the EQ bands, but in the case of an in-line console, on which it may possible to switch the shelving EQ into one channel path and then switch the two mids into the other, the two mids will generally be given an extended range, allowing them the facility to cover the entire audio spectrum between them.

The fixed bandwidth or Q of sweep-mid equalisers is inevitably a compromise: too low a Q will affect an excessively wide a range of frequencies, while too high a Q will sound harsh or peaky if any degree of boost is applied. Unfortunately, different material benefits from different levels of Q. This is evident, for example, if you mike up an electric guitar and there is a sharply defined honk caused by cabinet resonance at, say, 500Hz, and you then apply some cut at a bandwidth just wide enough to tame the resonance without seriously affecting the sound outside that range. On the other hand, if you just want to add a little boost to the mid-range in general, then a lower Q would sound smoother.

Some mid-priced desks get around this restriction by offering a two-position bandwidth switch to provide two different characteristics, one moderate and one sharp, which is clearly a more useful setup. But the logical conclusion of this line of thought would be to provide an extra variable control in place of the switch so that the equaliser could be made fully parametric. There are a few mid-priced analogue consoles out there that include one or more fully parametric mid sections, but in most cases it's true to say that, if you need to apply parametric EQ, you'll have to patch in an external parametric equaliser.

Digital Equalisers

The potential of digital equalisation is enormous because, with digital models, it's possible to create filter responses by mathematical means that are well-nigh impossible to reproduce using analogue circuitry. The equalisation in digital mixers tends to be modelled on its analogue counterpart, though it's quite common to find four fully parametric bands in even a modest digital console – something you'd only ever find in very high-end analogue desks. The subjective quality of digital desk equalisers varies enormously, and with some designs it appears that much more boost or cut has to be applied in order to achieve the same subjective results as would be obtained with a similarly specified analogue equaliser. This has led many to speculate that the phase response of the equaliser may be concerned as much with the subjective effect of an equaliser as with its frequency response.

EQ And Perception

Check any textbook and you'll see the limits of human hearing quoted as being around 50Hz to 20kHz, though those same books will also point out that very few individuals, other than young children, can hear pitches anything like as high as 20kHz. A more realistic figure might be around 15kHz for an adult, decreasing as the years pass. What is puzzling, though (and this area provides scope enough for a book in its own right), is that, even if your measured hearing response starts to fall off at well below 20kHz, you can still hear the effect of EQ applied at the top end of the spectrum, where you would not expect to be able to hear any change.

The mystery deepens further when reputable studio engineers claim to be able to differentiate between two otherwise identical audio circuits, in which one has been modified to handle frequencies up to 50kHz and one handles frequencies only up to 30kHz. In theory both limits are well above the threshold of human perception, so it seems that sounds which exceed the audible spectrum have a way of influencing what we perceive as audible. It is for this reason that most audiophile quality studio equipment, including mixing consoles, has a frequency response extending to 40kHz or beyond. Of course, many digital mixing consoles are limited by their sampling rate to a frequency response of around 20kHz, though the current move towards 24-bit 96kHz (or 88.2kHz) audio will double this figure and bring it more into line with that of analogue.

The Effect Of EQ

At heart, no matter how complicated it becomes, EQ is still really just a frequency-selective volume control, and yet its subjective effect on the sound is often more profound than this simple description might lead you to expect. In less civilised times human beings relied on their hearing for survival, so when it comes to noting how much of your attention will be grabbed by a sound in a mix it's a good idea to try to analyse what we hear in different natural situations.

Some researchers believe that, in the Earth's atmosphere, low frequencies travel slightly faster than high frequencies, and so the greater the distance between the source of the sound and the listener the more delay there is between the low frequencies (which arrive first) and the upper harmonics which follow. If this is true then sounds existing higher up the auditory spectrum experience greater delay, and so in effect the harmonic structure of the sound becomes progressively more smeared as it travels. The atmosphere also absorbs high frequencies more readily than low ones, and so the further away the source of the sound the less bright it sounds by the time it reaches us.

Clearly we've become accustomed to sound behaving like this – our brains don't recognise the phase distortion as such; they just recognise the sound as being distant. By the same token, louder sounds that have little or no phase smearing are perceived as being close by. With recorded sounds, however, we're faced with the problem that all sounds travel the same distance – if the hi-fi speakers are three metres from the listener then that's how far the sound travels. What we need is a way of faking the illusion of distance or closeness, and in this the correct use of EQ can help.

Level And Phase

We already know that EQ acts like a selective volume control, affecting only certain parts of the audio spectrum depending on the frequency characteristics of the filter circuit used. However, it's well known to circuit designers that EQ doesn't change only the level of specific parts of the spectrum: it also changes the phase of the affected frequencies relative to those that aren't being cut or boosted. Because of this phase characteristic the top cut equaliser creates an effect similar to that obtained by increasing the distance between the listener and the sound source.

This is almost certainly why brightening up a sound makes is seem closer, while winding off some high end makes it seem more distant. In practice, every design of EQ affects the audio spectrum and phase response in a different way, and (leaving aside technical criteria such as noise and distortion) this probably at least partly explains why some EQs have a more natural, musical sound than others.

Impressions Of Loudness

It's an established fact that the human hearing curve isn't flat but is more sensitive to mid-range sounds than to frequencies at the extreme high and low ends of the audio spectrum. Again, we don't notice this because we've been hearing things in this way all of our lives. However, as the level of sound increases, so the mid boost of our hearing system becomes reduced, with the result that high- and low-frequency sounds seem proportionally louder. This is yet another of those interesting physiological factors that can be exploited, and is used to fool the ear into believing that it is perceiving something not entirely true. For example, if we know that extreme high and low frequencies stand out more when we listen to loud music, we can create the impression of loudness at lower levels by attenuating the mid range and boosting the high- and low-frequency ends of the audio spectrum. The loudness button on a stereo system does exactly this, and if you look at the graphic EQs used in a night club or on a PA system you'll often see them set up to show a smile-shaped curve to promote the illusion of loudness and power. Of course, this works just as well in the studio, although it's most effective just to treat some of the sounds in a mix in order to maintain some kind of contrast between the different sounds.

To Cut Or Boost?

In general, the less EQ boost you use the more natural the final sound will be. The human ear is far more tolerant of EQ cut than it is of boost, especially at high Q settings, and so instead of adding lots of top to critical sounds such as vocals in order to get them to sit at the front of the mix you could try applying high-end cut to other sounds in the mix that are conflicting with the vocal.

Some classical purists might say that you don't need EQ at all, but in the real world of pop recording, in which the emphasis is placed on appropriate rather than accurate sounds, equalisation has become a way of life. The close miking of drums was originally tried in an attempt to cut down on spill from other instruments, but now it's become the normal pop drum sound. EQ plays a very large part in creating the modern drum sound, but because we're not usually trying to emulate the original acoustic drum sound the EQ is used in a creative context rather than in a corrective one.

Separating Sounds

EQ can be used in many ways, but one of its most popular applications is in separating two similar sounds within a mix where the degree of overlap is causing the sound to become confused or muddled. If, for example, two sounds are fighting it out in the same part of the spectrum, a peaking equaliser can be used to add a degree of bite to one sound at one frequency while the other sound can be peaked up at a different frequency. Similarly, the top or bottom end of a sound can be 'trimmed' to avoid conflict, a typical example being the acoustic rhythm guitar in a pop mix, where the bottom end can get confused with the vocals, the drums or even the bass guitar. Here you can roll off quite a lot of the bottom end without spoiling the sound of the guitar, though if you listen to it in isolation it will probably sound rather thin. This introduces an important fact about EQ that I'll return to later: it's not what something sounds like in isolation that counts but how it sounds in the context of the mix as a whole.

When To EQ

As a general rule, equalisation should be employed only after all efforts have been made to obtain the best sound at source. What's more, there's a huge subjective difference in sound between a budget equaliser and a top-quality studio equaliser, so if you have to work with a budget EQ, or the EQ section built into your desk, you'll probably have to use it very sparingly if the overall sound isn't to suffer, especially if you want to make changes in the critical 800Hz–4kHz region, at which level the human ear is very sensitive. Though the character of a really nice equaliser is difficult to quantify, the best equalisers allow you to make more drastic changes without the sound appearing unnatural, nasal or harsh.

A combination of cut and boost is required in most cases, but it's always best to use the EQ bypass switch to flip back and forth between the equalised and unequalised sounds to ensure that you really have improved matters. Equally, if you feel the need to EQ an instrument in isolation, check it again with all tracks playing to make sure that the setting you're using works in the rest of the mix as a whole. More often than not you'll have to make further adjustments. Once again, it is important that your sounds are good at the outset – EQ is an invaluable ally in shaping well-recorded sounds, but even the best equalisers experience difficulties when faced with poorly recorded material.

Locating Sounds

Probably the best way to familiarise yourself with the audio spectrum is to check out some common musical sounds and identify which part of the audible range they occupy. Try feeding a commercial CD through your equaliser and applying a few decibels of boost and sweep through the frequency range to hear how different sounds and instruments are picked out. The low-frequency limit of an instrument is usually quite easy to define, as an instrument can't produce a pitch below the fundamental frequency of its lowest note. However, the high-frequency end is somewhat less identifiable because nearly all sounds include harmonics that extend right to the top end of the audio spectrum and beyond, and even though the level of these harmonics is probably very low they're

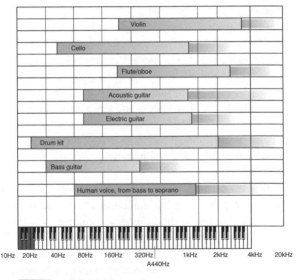

Harmonics of the instrument

Figure 3.6: Chart of common sound frequencies

still very important in defining the sound and creating the impression of clarity. The most useful method I can use to illustrate this is to pick a ball-park range and show where most of the audio energy from a particular source resides. It's up to you to try EQ'ing above these frequencies to find out how much the sound is affected. A flute produces a relatively pure tone, for example, though the breath noise harmonics extend to the top of the audio spectrum and will respond to high-frequency EQ. Figure 3.6 shows a few common sounds in chart form so that their frequency ranges can be compared.

Drums

The bass drum puts out most of its energy in a narrow band between 50Hz and 150Hz depending on how it is tuned, but the attack transients reach right up into the upper-mid range. This can be confirmed by applying some EQ boost to a bass drum sound at around the range of 4–6kHz, where the difference in the attack characteristic is very noticeable. The usual trick when recording pop music is to add weight by boosting between 70 and 90Hz.

Drums are a special case when it comes to equalisation because the accepted pop and rock drum sound is not that of a natural kit. What's more, if you include the cymbals then a kit can cover the entire audio spectrum.

The trick is to make the drums sound both bright and solid but not too thick.

A close-miked bass drum without EQ will often sound less than ideal, though occasionally you get a great sound straight off. Most often there is a need to add definition to the hit, plus a degree of low-frequency weight. For a straightforward, punchy sound a little boost at 80Hz will almost always improve matters, but to get a deeper sound without the end result being too boomy try adding around 10dB of boost with your shelving bass control (most consoles have their bass controls at 50 or 60Hz) and then wind in a similar amount of cut at around 220Hz using the lower-mid control. The two controls should work together to produce a narrow area of low-frequency boost rather than the wide, uncontrollable boost that is obtained by using the low EQ on its own. The result is a kick sound with a lot of low weight.

To add definition to the beater impact, try boosting the upper-mid range between 3.5 and 6kHz and choose the final setting by ear. A wooden beater is far better than a felt one for producing a modern kick drum sound, and the slap can be further enhanced by taping a piece of thin plastic on the drum head on the exact spot at which the beater impacts. Credit cards work splendidly for this!

Toms may be handled in much the same way as bass drums, with boost (using the lower-mid sweep control) applied in the 80–120Hz region, depending on the size and type of tom. Careful adjustment of the upper-mid control can help pick out the stick impact, and if the tom rings on too much, or if it rings in sympathy with other drums, you can usually afford to roll off quite a lot of bass without the result sounding thin in final mix. I often use a gated side-chain filter in Key-Listen mode for this because of its very sharp response – I know that isn't exactly for what it was intended, but it works perfectly! This kind of corrective EQ is invariably more effective than applying too much damping to the drum.

Snare drums are quite unpredictable, and you never quite know how they're going to sound until you've miked them up and listened to the result over the monitors. The sound can be fattened by boosting the 90–140Hz band, while the bite can usually be located in the 3–7kHz region. When searching for the right area, it's easiest to apply full boost and then tune to find the appropriate pitch. Once you've found it, you can then reduce the degree of boost until you have an acceptable sound. If the drum still doesn't sound crisp enough, try switching to a capacitor mic or patching in an exciter.

When recording to analogue, it's always best to record cymbals at a low level to prevent the tape from overloading, and keep in mind that they always cut through louder than you expect. Brightness can be added by using the shelving high EQ control, or you can tune the upper-mid control until you find a sweet spot. In general cymbals are recorded as part of the overhead mic mix, and in some cases it can help to roll off the bass end quite significantly to prevent the drum sounds picked up by the overhead mics from obstructing those picked up by the close mics.

Bass Guitars

Whether the bass guitar is DI'd or miked during recording, the equalisation on a typical console can be used to create a wide range of tonal characteristics. (I'm assuming the use of console with four-band EQ and two sweep mids, but it is possible to use an external graphic or parametric equaliser to achieve the same result.) The lowest note on the conventionally tuned four-string electric bass guitar is 41Hz, but the higher notes contain significant energy up to 2–3kHz.

Boosting at around 80Hz can be used to pull out the low bass, while boosting between 500Hz and 800Hz adds a nicely aggressive bite. Boosting higher up the spectrum tends to bring out the finger noise and little else, so if you're after a bright sound try to get it as close as you can at source. The tone produced by a bass guitar has a lot to do with playing technique, and no amount of EQ will compensate for weak finger technique. A touch of low-mid cut at around 200–250Hz can sometimes be effective in combination with a little low-end boost – this warms up the low bass end without allowing the low-mid area to become uncontrollably boomy. On the other hand, applying low mid-boost in a crowded mix might actually produce a more confident bass sound.

Bass synths can be treated in much the same way as bass guitars, though their ability to produce higher harmonics means that EQ at higher frequencies will also be effective. Be cautious when using very bright bass synth sounds, however, as they can very easily fill up all the space in a mix, leaving the whole thing sounding congested.

The traditional pipe organ goes an octave lower than the bass guitar, down to 20Hz or so, descending into the region where sounds are felt rather than heard. High organ notes, on the other hand, generate a significant amount of energy as far up the spectrum as 8kHz and beyond. Synthesiser sounds can also go this low, or even lower, but there's little point in adding energy at 20Hz when few domestic loudspeaker systems extend far below 50Hz.

Electric Guitars

The electric guitar has a starting point of 82Hz, one octave higher than the bass guitar, and because of the restricted range of electric guitar speakers there's little energy above 4kHz. Even so, it's a mistake to draw too many conclusions from the upper limit of any sound because EQ applied above this arbitrary limit will almost certainly have some audible effect.

If you need to add warmth to the sound of an electric guitar, concentrate on the area between 125Hz and 200Hz. There's no point adding boost much below this region as the lowest note's fundamental frequency is 82Hz. Bass boost will only bring up the cabinet boom and make the overall sound muddy, and it could also conflict with the bass guitar. Equally importantly, boosting the bass end will accentuate any mains hum in the signal (most guitar pickups, especially single-coil jobs, pick up a surprising amount of hum).

Try shifting the 3–4kHz section of the audio spectrum to add attack to the sound, but don't add any really high-end boost unless the guitar is DI'd as there's not much coming out of a guitar speaker above this range.

All you'll do is accentuate the background noise, and if the guitar is being used with an overdrive sound then this will tend to turn buzzy or fizzy.

In a congested mix, two similar-sounding guitars can be separated by adding bite at different frequencies (for example, one guitar at 3kHz and one at 4kHz). However, this is rarely as successful as obtaining a different sound at source. What may help is using two different amplifiers or pre-amp settings while recording the two parts. It also makes sense to use different types of guitar – for example, one with single-coil pickups and one with humbuckers. If you're miking the guitar amp, try using different mics for the different parts – a dynamic for one take and a capacitor for the other will make a noticeable difference, even if the guitar, amp and player remain the same.

The Piano

The piano must be recorded using good, properly positioned mics or no amount of EQ will restore the natural sound. Bass can be enhanced by boosting at around 90–150Hz, while attack can be brought out by bringing up the 4–6kHz area of the audio spectrum. 'Air' can be added by applying wide-band boost at around 15kHz. If the sound is boomy, look for the offending area between 250Hz and 350Hz and apply enough cut to keep it under control. Because the piano is such a natural instrument, it pays to use less EQ and to concentrate instead on correctly positioning suitable mics when recording.

Electronic sample-based pianos can be equalised in the same way, though many models offer such a range of piano sounds that equalisation may be unnecessary.

Vocals

Vocals can range from around 80Hz to 1kHz, depending on the style and sex of the performer. Again, there's a significant amount of energy above that range, which is why live-mic manufacturers often build in a presence peak at the 3–4kHz mark, and de-essers have to function at between 5kHz and 10kHz to remove sibilance.

Always use a pop shield when recording vocals, as no amount of EQ will fix popping once it's on tape. Try to get as near to the required sound as possible without resorting to EQ by selecting the most sympathetic mic. General brightening can be achieved by using the shelving high EQ control, but listen out for sibilance. Boosting lower down, at 1–2kHz, gives the vocals a rather honky, cheap sound and so is not recommended, other than as a special effect. Presence can be added by adding just a little boost at 3–4kHz using the upper-mid sweep equaliser, but be sparing in this as the natural character of the voice can easily be lost. In a mix of backing vocals, rolling off a touch of bass often helps the sound blend in better with the rest of the mix.

Brass And Strings

As with vocals, brass and stringed instruments also tend to occupy the mid range of the audio spectrum, typically 80Hz–1kHz – unless you count the tuba, of course, in which case you can subtract almost an octave from the bottom of that figure. Brass and stringed instruments work on entirely different principles but they respond to equalisation in similar ways. Between 1kHz and 3.5kHz the sound can become nasal or honky, and a little subtle cutting in this region can sweeten things up. To add high-end sizzle, move up to the 6–10kHz band and try a little boost there, but don't overdo it or the sound will become spitty. For a warm pad sound from string samples, brass samples and synth patches, roll off a little top and add a hint of boost between 300Hz and 400Hz.

Bright Sounds

Few instruments produce a great amount of energy at the upper end of the audio spectrum but the piccolo and xylophone come the closest, having a marked presence in the 600Hz–5kHz range. The upper harmonics of cymbals, bell trees, triangles and other high-end percussion extend well beyond the limit of human hearing.

Sampled and synthesised sounds haven't been included in this because they can cover whatever range the electrical circuitry is capable of supporting, which in theory can be the entire audio spectrum.

Useful EQ Frequencies

Mains hum occurs at 50Hz and multiples thereof, so applying cut at 50Hz and 100Hz using a narrowly tuned parametric can help to remove hum from a recording without significantly affecting the overall sound. However, you will need a good-quality equaliser to achieve this as a cheap model might ring noticeably at the frequency to which it's tuned, even in cut mode. A third-octave graphic may also help in this situation, but other types of equaliser are likely to have a range that is too wide, which means that some bass sounds will be seriously affected. Expect some change to the wanted sound, though, especially if you need to apply a lot of cut.

The best anti-hum filters exist as software plug-ins for computer workstations. Some packages are capable of automatically tracking small variations in the hum frequency while deploying additional filters to deal with the harmonics. There may also be a facility by which the filter cut is less severe when the sound is loud enough to mask the hum, as the less EQ cut you use the less audible any side-effects will be. There are also digital hardware hum filters that work on a similar principle.

Bass Drums And Bass Guitars
Punchiness at around 80Hz, definition at 2.5–5kHz.

Electric Guitars
Boxy at around 200Hz, harsh or nasal at 1–2kHz. Brightness at 3–6kHz.

Acoustic Guitars
Muddy or boomy between 200Hz and 500Hz, nasal at 1kHz, zingy at 5–7kHz. Add a little 'air' EQ to open up the top end.

Air
To add more top-end zing to a clean guitar or vocal sound try using a shelving high control, or better still a parametric with a low Q set to boost at around 12–15kHz. The latter setting helps add air to virtually any sound that contains high-frequency harmonics. Experiment with applying broad-band boost in the air

band as this is a very useful production trick, both for EQ'ing single sounds and for treating mixes.

Vocals

Boomy at 150Hz, nasal at 1kHz, sibilant at 3–6kHz, air at 8–15kHz. Avoid excessive use of EQ when aiming for a natural sound.

4 PATCHING AND PATCHBAYS

Most of the connections in a typical studio or live sound setup are rigged through the mixer, but there needs to be some provision available to make changes to some of the system connections so that you don't have to crawl around the back of the mixer and effects rack with a torch. There may be many such audio connections even in the small home studio, so the only practical approach is to bring all of the regularly used inputs and outputs to a patchbay so that they can be conveniently patched together using short signal leads.

Professional patchbays use high-reliability miniature Bantam jack plugs and sockets, often with gold-plated contacts to provide a flexible and durable (if highly expensive) patching system. Budget semi-pro systems are much more realistically priced and tend to be based on readily available mass-produced plastic sockets, which accept standard quarter-inch instrument-style jack plugs. Both unbalanced and balanced versions are available. This is a convenient format for the musician, as most musical instruments rely on quarter-inch jack connections.

The physical patchbay format usually consists of a rack-mountable 1U panel, generally with two rows of between 16 and 24 sockets and each socket on the top row paired with the socket below it. Traditionally, the top row of sockets is for outputs and the bottom row for inputs. A typical patching system runs the most commonly used inputs and outputs to the patchbay, where they can be connected as desired using short jack-to-jack leads. Patchbays are most commonly used to gain access to console line inputs, aux sends and returns, equipment inputs and outputs and insert points, but not all are wired in the same way. Any patchbay socket pair wired to handle an insert point must be normalised.

Normalising

Figure 4.1 shows how the pairs of sockets in an unbalanced patchbay are wired, though the concept is similar for a balanced patchbay. If your console has balanced ins and outs then it's sensible to make this part of your patchbay balanced as well, though the insert points on a typical home-recording analogue console will invariably be unbalanced. The signal ground connections are often permanently linked between the socket pairs, and there may be a wire or track link on the printed circuit that normalises the two sockets. (Normalising means that, when no plug is inserted, the top and bottom sockets are automatically connected.)

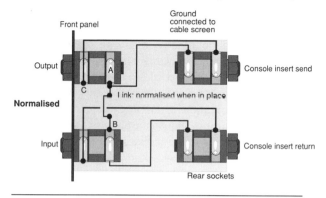

Normalised

- Front panel
- Output
- A
- C
- Link: normalised when in place
- B
- Input
- Ground connected to cable screen
- Console insert send
- Console insert return
- Rear sockets

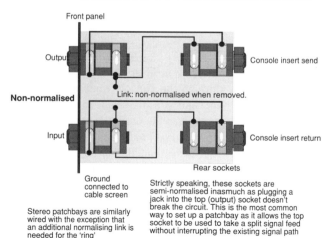

Non-normalised

- Front panel
- Output
- Link: non-normalised when removed.
- Input
- Console insert send
- Console insert return
- Rear sockets
- Ground connected to cable screen

Stereo patchbays are similarly wired with the exception that an additional normalising link is needed for the 'ring' connection of the jack

Strictly speaking, these sockets are semi-normalised inasmuch as plugging a jack into the top (output) socket doesn't break the circuit. This is the most common way to set up a patchbay as it allows the top socket to be used to take a split signal feed without interrupting the existing signal path

Figure 4.1: Patchbay socket pair

basic Mixers

Another popular normalising system is to have each pair of sockets mounted on their own separate PCBs (Printed Circuit Boards), with another pair of identically spaced sockets at the back to carry the rear connection. These boards can be easily removed and replaced in one of two orientations, so that either pair of sockets can be at the front. The circuit board is designed so that the sockets are either normalised or not, depending on the orientation of the circuit board. If you're not sure which way is which, try plugging an instrument such as a synth into one of the rear sockets and plug the other rear socket into an amplifier. If you get a sound then the sockets are normalised; if you don't, they're not.

Normalising is necessary at insert points to maintain the signal flow through the console when nothing is plugged into them, and you may want to normalise other connections, such as the output of your console which feeds the input of a DAT machine, depending on the complexity of your system. This means that your most regularly used signal path is available without the need to insert patch leads and also that you can still get at the mixer output or DAT machine input by using patch leads if necessary.

The most commonly used semi-pro patchbays are fitted

with jack sockets on the rear so that other parts of the system can be easily connected. Other versions are available that allow cables to be soldered directly to the rear of the patchbay – in theory, minimising the number of connections produces a cleaner signal path. Using sockets is more flexible, however, as you may want to make changes to your patching system as your studio setup expands.

In Figure 4.1, contacts A carry the signal while contacts C provide the signal ground. The other set of contacts, B, are normally found only on the bottom row of sockets, and it is these, in conjunction with the link (shown as a dotted line), which normalise the sockets. Actually, as there is only a switched contact on the lower socket, it would be more correct to say that the patch bay is semi-normalised. What does this mean in practice?

When no plugs are inserted, contact B is mechanically switched to contact A so that the signal coming in on the back of the top socket is routed via the link directly into the lower socket. This completes the circuit, so that the console's insert send is routed directly back to its insert return.

However, if a plug is inserted into the lower socket then

the contacts open and no signal flows along the link, and if the top socket is patched to the input and the bottom socket to the output of and effects device then contact B opens and the entire signal is diverted via the effects unit before being returned to the mixer. Switch contacts are not fitted to the top socket because this arrangement provides a convenient way of splitting a signal on those occasions when you might want to take a feed from a mixer channel without breaking the normal signal flow. A typical application of this feature would be to split a signal, delay one part of it (with a DDL, for example) and then pan that part to one side and the unprocessed sound to the other. Without a patchbay of this kind you would need a splitter box, or a split lead at the very least, to perform this kind of task.

Ergonomics

Another important role played by the patchbay is that of simply locating all of the inputs and outputs of the effects units, console inputs and aux sends and returns where they are conveniently at hand to the user. In fact, any type of audio connection that you might want to access on a regular basis can be arranged and routed via a patchbay. If the patchbay is handling simple inputs and outputs rather than insert points, you should un-normalise the sockets; failure to do this would result in the inputs and outputs of equipment becoming joined when no plugs were inserted into the patchbay, and this could well cause the gear in question to oscillate. Depending on the type of patchbay, this may involve removing a wire link or making sure that the reversible circuit board is the right way around.

Side-Chain Inputs

One other connection which is handy to bring out to a patchbay is the key or side-chain input, which is found on the backs of some gates and compressors. Connecting these inputs, however, is not always as straightforward as it might seem, so before doing anything it's important to check the manual to see exactly how the side-chain socket is wired on the equipment. Sometimes the sockets are straightforward inputs which are selectable via a front-panel switch, which is no problem, but on other occasions they may be wired in the same way as an insert send/return, in which case you'll have to use a normalised pair of sockets. Most reputable rack-mounted gear is designed to be used in conjunction with a patchbay, so if you haven't got the information you need to bring the key inputs out to your patchbay then don't be afraid to phone the manufacturer or distributor and ask for more details.

Wiring

When wiring to and from the patchbay you should use separate screened cables, but for unbalanced insert points where the distance is not more than a few feet you can generally use a twin-cored screened cable, in which one core carries the incoming signal and the other the outgoing signal. The screen connection needs only to be connected to one of the two jacks feeding the patchbay, as the two socket grounds are linked in the patchbay itself. Figure 4.2 shows how an insert patch point is wired. Foil-screened cable works well and is easy to strip and solder, though any high-quality co-axial cable is fine. With budget recording equipment, console inserts are generally connected via a TRS stereo jack at the mixer end, so this method of wiring is most convenient.

If you find that your desk behaves oddly and has a tendency to hum once the patch bay is wired up, this may be due to ground loop problems. Check your wiring to ensure that you don't have multiple earths connected to any single piece of equipment (see the section on ground loops for more information on how to tackle this irritating problem). As a rule, don't join the cable grounds to any metalwork or to the mains earth, and with balanced connections it's usually wise to leave the screen disconnected at one end of the cable. Don't

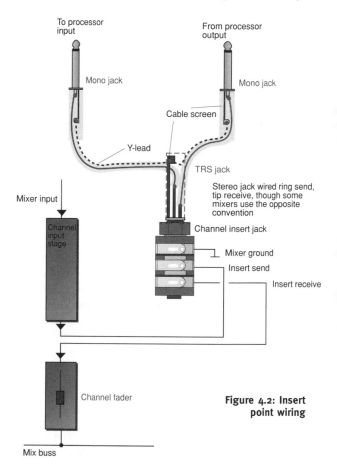

To processor input

From processor output

Mono jack

Mono jack

Cable screen

Y-lead

TRS jack

Stereo jack wired ring send, tip receive, though some mixers use the opposite convention

Mixer input

Channel input stage

Channel insert jack

Mixer ground

Insert send

Insert receive

Channel fader

Figure 4.2: Insert point wiring

Mix buss

wire speaker signals to your patchbay as you could connect them to signal inputs by mistake, and the high signal level could cause severe damage.

Routing And Patching

The roles of the various signal processors and effects used in audio production are fully described elsewhere in this book, but it's not always obvious where they should be patched into the signal chain to give the best results.

If you're using a cassette multitracker then you have few options, but if you move up to a separate multitrack recorder and mixer you will find yourself confronted by aux sends, insert points and mixing consoles with routing systems so advanced that they rival those of professional desks. Even if you've read the rest of this book and know the basic ground rules, there will often be a better way of doing things if you stop and think about it.

I've already grouped outboard equipment into the categories of effects or processors, according to their function and design. You might think that this seems pedantic, especially when most boxes that don't actually produce noise in their own right are usually referred to as processors, but it does help avoid patching mistakes.

As I mentioned earlier, the main reason for separating boxes in this way is that there are certain restrictions on how processors can be connected, while effects (or FX, as they tend to be written) enjoy a little more flexibility. Processors take in a signal, do something to it and produce a modified version of the signal at the output socket. Processors include equalisers, compressors/limiters, expanders/gates, panners and equipment which influences single-ended noise reduction.

Effects are designed to be added to an existing signal. Remember that, if you're not quite sure whether a box is an effect or a processor, there are two simple checks you can make. Firstly, does the box rely on some type of delay circuitry to work? If so, it's almost certainly an effect. Secondly, does it have a mix control or mix parameter? Again, if it does it's likely to be an effect. The only slightly ambiguous boxes are exciters or enhancers, but these are best thought of as processors. Echo units, delay lines, reverbs, chorus/flangers, pitch shifters and phasers are all effects.

A potential dilemma arises when dealing with multi-effects boxes because most can function as either effects or processors, and a multi-effects patch might comprise both! If you set up a patch by which processors feed into effects then treat the whole patch as an effect.

However, if you have a chain of processors with no effects (for example, a compressor followed by an equaliser) then treat the combination as a processor and patch it via an insert point.

Routing Rules

On a modern mixing console, the post-fade aux sends (commonly known as *effects sends*) allow some of the signal passing through a mixer channel to be sent to an effects unit, such as a reverb or delay device. Using a patchbay makes these devices much easier to connect. The output from the effects device is then brought back into the mixer through a spare channel or an effects return (which is really just another channel, albeit without the frills) to be mixed in with the original sound. Again, effects returns and spare line inputs should be made accessible from your patchbay. Of course, stereo effects will take up two channels or returns unless your mixer has dedicated stereo aux returns, and to keep the effect in stereo the two returns must be panned hard left and right. Because each channel has its own aux send level controls the same effects unit can be used by several channels simultaneously. The aux send controls are merely knobs which introduce either more or less effect, enabling the user to set up different levels of effect for each channel. When the channel fader is turned down the effects level changes accordingly.

Under normal circumstances only effects should be patched in via the aux send return system, and I make no apology for repeating this as it's a very important point. If you were to do the same with a processor, such as an EQ unit, you'd just be adding EQ'd sound to the original sound, which in effect would dilute the effect of the EQ, often with unpredictable results. This is bad enough with an analogue desk, but on a digital desk, where there is a delay of a few thousandths of a second between signals going into the desk and coming out again, the effects of routing a signal to the same destination via two different routes can lead to very obvious comb filtering, which makes the sound appear 'phasey'.

Another popular method of patching external boxes is to use the channel, group and master insert points, all of which may be brought out to normalised patchbay points. Processors should always be connected via insert points or patched between the output of one piece of line level gear and the input of another. However, effects may also be patched into insert points, as long as you need the effect only on that particular channel or group of channels. If you plug an effect into an insert point, you'll need to use its own mix control to set the dry/effect balance. If you plug an effect into an aux send, you generally set it to produce a completely wet sound. For ease of reference, I've condensed some of the main routing information into a series of short points.

- Insert points are invariably presented as stereo jacks wired to carry both the send and return signals, so if you don't have a patchbay you'll need to use a Y-lead with a stereo jack at one end and two mono jacks at the other. These can be obtained commercially if you don't like doing any soldering yourself.

- Processors must be used 'in-line' with a signal and not in the effects send/return loop.

- Most processors work at line level, so you can't plug a mic directly into them. The correct way to compress a mic signal, for example, is to patch the compressor into the insert point of the mixer channel, which comes after the mic amp stage. This doesn't apply to mic channel processors that combine a mic amp with one or more processors.

- If an effect is used via the aux/send return system it is customary to set the effects unit's dry/effect ratio to effect only, so as to allow the console's aux send controls to govern the balance of the effect.

- If an effect is used via an insert point it is normal to use the effect unit's dry/effect ratio to control the effect balance.

- Some effects, such as phasing and flanging, rely on a precise effect/dry balance, which may be better accomplished in the effects unit itself. In this case, either patch the effects unit into an insert point or, if you must use the aux/send system, either de-route the channel from the stereo mix to kill the dry signal or feed the effects unit from a pre-fade (foldback) send and turn the channel fader right down.

- To use a mono-in/stereo-out effects unit (such as reverb or stereo delay) via insert points, simply route one output of the unit to the insert return of the channel which feeds it and the other to the insert return of a free adjacent channel. Match the levels and then pan one track hard left and the other hard right for maximum stereo effect.

- To use a stereo-in/stereo-out FX unit via insert points, use two adjacent mixer channels panned hard left and right.

- To treat a whole mix with, for example, EQ or compression, patch the processor into the master insert points. This places your unit in the signal path just before the master stereo faders, which means that, if you're using a compressor, it won't try to fight you if you introduce a fade-out. By the same token, any noise generated by the processor will also be faded as you pull the faders down.

- If you don't have master insert points, you can patch a processor between the mixer's stereo out and the input to your stereo mastering recorder; however, if you want to execute fades with a compressor patched in you'll need to do them using the input level control on the mastering machine, not on the desk. You'll also need to monitor the output of the master recorder to hear the effect of the fade.

Advanced Routing

If you want to process a group then the group insert points are the only way in. A typical application might be to compress a stereo backing vocal mix, or even a drum mix, which means using a stereo compressor patched into a group pair. Don't forget to set the compressor to stereo link mode in this instance.

If you want to compress or otherwise process a line-level signal, the obvious thing to do is to patch in the processor via the channel insert points. However, on most semi-pro desks the insert points are unbalanced, and there may be an advantage in first feeding the line-level signal through the processor and then plugging the output of the processor into the mixer's balanced line input. One advantage of using balanced connections is that there is less chance of picking up ground-loop hum.

Similarly, if you have enough spare line inputs, you might find it better to use these for effects returns, where you can maintain a balanced connection from the effect output to the mixer input.

Lateral Thinking

Catering for every patching possibility means a lot of patchbays, a lot of cable and a lot of plugs. On top of the obvious cost, patchbays invariably compromise the quality of your audio signal to some extent simply because of the additional cabling and plug/socket connections through which your signal has to travel. Unless you design your system very carefully, you can easily pick up ground-loop hum, and although this may at first be very low-level, it soon adds up when you have a number of effects and processors running together.

Normalised patchbay sockets used to handle inserts invariably attract corrosion and grease over a period of time, which can result in audible signal distortion and, eventually, intermittent connections. This situation can be improved by treating the socket contacts with an advanced contact cleaner such as Deoxit. Don't use cheap cleaning sprays, as these tend to leave a greasy film that attracts dust.

Although patchbays are invaluable, it pays to plan your system so as to keep patching at a minimum. By considering how your system will actually be used, you can usually avoid connecting every single item through a patchbay. For example, many modern mixers have six or even eight aux send busses, so unless you have more than eight effects units you could opt to permanently wire your effects directly to the aux sends and returns of your desk. This prevents both unnecessary patching and expenditure, and maintains the best possible signal quality. If you have fewer effects units than you have sends, you could usefully wire up the spare sends to a patchbay so that you could plug in visiting effects.

If your studio is for your own rather than commercial use, you could permanently plug your favourite vocal compressor into, say, channel one of your console and always use this channel to record your lead vocal. If you make sure that you always record your lead vocal onto tape track one in every session, you can bring it back through the same compressor without having to repatch. The same philosophy can be applied to gates. If you only ever use them after recording you could connect them between your multitrack and desk rather than via the insert points, which would enable you to use balanced wiring (if your gates and tape machine are balanced). This maximises signal quality, reduces the risk of hum and, again, saves on wiring and patchbays. Of course, you would have to plan your sessions more carefully, so that anything that needs gating is recorded onto the tape tracks that correspond to your gates, but after just a little thought about your own working methods you'll probably find that you can cut the complexity of your patchbay down to around 25% or less than that of a full patchbay system.

The same applies to exciters or enhancers – if you always enhance the whole stereo mix without adding any other overall processing, you could wire your enhancer directly into your console's stereo insert points. If you prefer to use it on just some parts of a mix and not others, however, you could instead wire it into a pair of group inserts.

If you're using a mixer that connects via standard jacks, and you've made a number of permanent routing decisions similar to those above, you might even be able to abandon the patchbay altogether because, on the rare occasion that you want to set up something out of the ordinary, you can always change the connections to the mixer. While this is inconvenient if you have to rearrange things every session, it's less of a problem if you only need to do it once in a while.

I must stress here that, if you want an efficient patchbay system, you will have to plan it carefully before you start connecting it up, and if you decide that you can manage without one you will still have to plan!

The following list suggests some of the connections that you could bring out to a patchbay and whether or not the normalising link should be left in. Those connections that are not insert points, but for which normalisation has been recommended, provide in effect new insert points between the pieces of equipment concerned. For example, the mixer group outs and multitrack line-ins would normally be connected, but inserting a patchbay between them will enable you to access the mixer outs and the recorder ins independently, as well as enabling you to insert processors directly between the mixer outs and the recorder inputs. This can be particularly useful with digital mixers, with which you may not get as many insert points as those provided on an analogue console.

SIGNAL	NORMALISED?
Channel insert points	Yes
Group insert points	Yes
Line inputs to desk	No
Line inputs to multitrack	Optional
Line outputs from multitrack	Optional
Line inputs to two-track	Optional
Line outputs from two-track	Optional
Effect sends from desk	No
Effect returns to desk	No
Input to effects	No
Outputs from effects	No
Key inputs	Consult manual

It is considered good practice to use a separate patchbay for MIDI signals on DIN connectors, and the same applies to gate pulses and control voltages if you have a collection of vintage analogue voltage-controlled synths. Mic inputs would normally be routed to a wall box rather than run to a patchbay and connected with balanced XLR plugs and sockets (as long as the mixer input is balanced).

Special Cases

So far I've covered all of the basic patchbay connections, but there are some less common situations that may have you scratching your head. For example, what happens if you have a gate with a key input that becomes active as soon as you plug in a jack? If you connect this to a patchbay the key input will be permanently active, and there's no easy wiring dodge to get around this. Fortunately, most reputable gates have a front-panel switch to activate the key input. If you have a model that won't co-operate, you'll have to resign yourself to visiting the back of the rack every once in a while.

The effects unit that has stereo inputs, but allows you to use it in mono only by plugging in one input, poses another problem. As soon as you connect both of its inputs to a patchbay it thinks you want to send it a

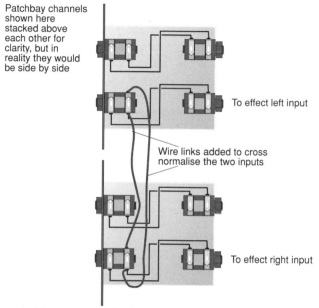

Patchbay channels shown here stacked above each other for clarity, but in reality they would be side by side

To effect left input

Wire links added to cross normalise the two inputs

To effect right input

In this arrangement, if only one input of a stereo effects unit is patched then the patchbay will automatically route the same signal to both inputs

Figure 4.3: Cross-normalising stereo inputs

stereo signal, so if you then send a mono signal to just one of the inputs you may find that only one channel works properly. To solve this problem you will need to create your own cross-normalising system between the two adjacent sockets handling the effects unit inputs, as shown in Figure 4.3. This involves simply soldering two short wire links, as shown in the diagram, so that, when either of the inputs is used on its own, the signal is also linked to the other input jack via the socket's normalising contacts. If both inputs are used, the unit reverts to normal stereo operation.

5 STUDIO MIXING

Watching a really skilled engineer at work can be an intimidating experience. The real experts can move along the desk pushing up the faders one at a time, having an almost perfectly balanced mix by the time they reach the end. Somehow they seem to have an instinct for balance, and what they achieve apparently magic we have to arrive at by hard work.

Before starting the mix it helps to organise logical groups of sounds into subgroups, which means that the mix can be handled with fewer faders. Most recordings have the drums spread over several tape tracks, and life is far easier if these are routed to a pair of adjacent group faders to form a stereo subgroup. Similarly, backing vocals can be assigned to subgroups along with any other sections that seem logical additions.

Keeping It Quiet

Routing the minimum number of channels that are strictly necessary to the mix buss will reduce mix buss noise. Most aux send controls don't have routing buttons, although if your console uses switching to swap an aux send between one of two busses there is another way, and the easiest way of explaining this is by example.

Let's assume that your console has a switch on it which allows one of the aux sends to be swapped between Aux 1 and Aux 3. If you connect your effect to Aux 1 but then set any channels on which the effect is not needed over to Aux 3 then the mix buss noise which will be contributed by the 'no effects' channels will be shunted to Aux 3 (which you're not using) rather than being sent to aux one, which is in use. On a large console, this can make a considerable difference in reducing the levels of background noise.

A similar arrangement applies to unused mixer channels. If you de-route these channels by making sure that all of the routing buttons are up (rather than simply muting the unused channels) then they won't add noise to your mix. Contrary to expectations, if you simply mute the channel some mix buss noise will still be added.

Finally, when you're connecting up your patchbay, it's important to try to keep mains wiring and mains power supply adaptors away from your signal wiring. If this is impossible and you cannot avoid them crossing, making sure that they do so only at right angles will minimise the risk of interference.

Balance

If the basic tracks have been recorded properly it should be possible to set up a reasonable initial balance without resorting to EQ. It's not necessary for effects to be added right from the outset, but it helps to have the necessary effects units patched in and ready for use, and some vocal reverb helps paint the picture. Switch the EQ to bypass on all channels on which it isn't being used and ensure that any unused mixer channels are not only muted but also unrouted – in other words, all of the routing buttons should be in their up position. This will prevent the channel from contributing to the mix buss noise of the console, and will help to achieve a quieter final mix. All unused aux sends should be set at level zero, and the loudest sends should be between three quarters and full up. Again, this will help to reduce noise. If your console has the ability to trim when it comes to mixdown then all console inputs should be trimmed using the PFL metering system. Likewise, all of your effects units should be checked to ensure that they're set to the correct input levels. If it's possible to route unused sends to an aux buss that isn't being used then this can reduce mix noise to a considerable degree, while any effect intended to process a single channel will produce the best audio quality if it's connected via the channel insert point.

Having attended to these basic niceties, my own personal method of working is to first sort out the drum and bass balance, but this should not be refined too much as the apparent balance will change once the rest of the instruments and voices are added to the mix. When the rhythm section starts to sound good, the remaining faders can be brought up one at a time until a reasonable overall balance has been achieved. It's only when all of the instruments are in place that you should start to worry about the finer points of EQ and balance, because things sound so different when they are heard in isolation.

Of course, some engineers and producers insist that the only possible way to work is to put all of the faders up to start with and then adjust for a balance. Don't be put off by this claim, however, because I've spoken to many well-regarded engineers and producers who admit that they don't have this natural gift for balance – they have to work just as hard as the rest of us!

Stereo Positioning
Once a reasonable balance has been achieved you can then start to work on the effects being used and

the stereo positioning of the different sounds. Bass drums, bass guitars and bass synths are invariably panned to the centre to anchor the mix and to spread the load of these high energy frequencies over both speakers. Similarly, lead vocals are usually positioned centre-stage because that's where we expect the vocalist to be.

The position of backing vocals is less rigid and can be split so that some are panned left and some right. They can be left in the centre, or they can all be grouped in one position off-centre. I like to hear different lines of backing vocals coming in from different sides, but this decision is purely artistic – there is no absolute right or wrong technique. If recorded vocals exhibit any sibilance problems, a de-esser should be patched in before proceeding.

Once the mix is almost there, it can be very helpful to listen to the balance from an adjacent room with the adjoining door left open. Although I can find no logical explanation for the phenomenon, any slight balance problems show up quite clearly when a mix is heard in this way, and most engineers and producers who have discovered this way of checking use it regularly. Figure 5.1 shows a typical panning arrangement for a pop song.

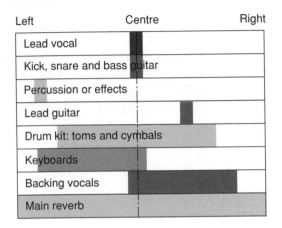

Figure 5.1: Typical stereo-panning scenario

Level Correction

A good mix will almost fly by itself, but some parts invariably need level corrections throughout the mix. Obvious examples are instrumental solos and changes in effects levels, but even on vocals with heavy compression it may still be necessary to adjust the occasional vocal phrase by a decibel or so to make it sit properly. If the mix is being conducted manually, the responsibility for the various fader adjustments can be delegated amongst the various members of the band. The settings of the levels should be clearly marked with a wax pencil, and each person involved in the mix should make a note of the tape counter positions at which levels have to be changed. Of course, if an automated mixing system is available then these changes can be handled automatically.

If the ending of a track requires a fade out, this may be performed manually or with an autofader. Fades are seldom shorter than 15 seconds and may be as long as 30, so it is important to ensure that there is enough recorded material to cover the duration of the fade. If you know in advance that the album is going to be compiled using a hard-disk editing system it might be wiser to leave the fades until the final editing stage, at which point they can be controlled more precisely and can be faded into true silence.

I've already covered some of the console settings that introduce noise, but we also have to consider noise that is part of the recorded sound. This can include breath noise from singers, hum and hiss from guitars and digital background noise from synths, samplers and drum machines. If sequenced MIDI instruments are being used, it is often possible to program level changes via MIDI. You should be careful here, however, as some instruments emit a more or less constant level of noise, regardless of the level of the voice playing.

You should always strive to use these machines as close to their maximum volume setting as is practical, as this will usually give the best signal-to-noise ratio. Likewise, it is possible to mute instruments via the sequencer, but this just stops the sequenced parts from playing and doesn't affect the background noise in any way.

Gates And Mutes

Gates and expanders are very effective in cleaning up electronic instruments, though care must be taken to match the release time of the gate to the sound being processed. In some cases it may be possible to use a pair of gates over a stereo subgroup, which has the advantage of requiring fewer gates. It must be remembered, though, that gates can only keep the noise down during pauses and can do nothing when signal is present.

Perhaps the most dramatic effect of MIDI muting or gating can be noticed right at the beginning of a song, where perfect silence reigns until the first note is played. In this case, it shouldn't be necessary to mute every short silence, but it's nevertheless a good idea to mute the vocal track during instrumental solos or bridge sections and to mute the lead guitar track both before and after a solo.

Muting a MIDI console can be very useful when you're trying to deal with source noise, and although it may take a little time to set up, the results are usually well worth the trouble. It's necessary to go through each tape track and set up the mute points individually, but once they're right they'll stay right every time you run the mix. If you can arrange muting and unmuting on a beat, it may help to disguise any discontinuity or change in noise level.

The mutes on most MIDI desks operate very quietly, but I know that on some models there is an audible click if many mutes are switched at the same time. If this is the case, it should be possible to work around the problem by using the mutes on the subgroups or master output faders rather than attempting to switch all of the channels at once.

Mix Processing

Producers tend to be divided when it comes to applying further processing to the overall stereo mix. The more puritanical might say that there is no need to process the mix once it's right, while others will insist on putting it through their favourite compressor, equaliser or exciter. There can be no definitive right or wrong method here – when producing pop music, the end always justifies the means, as long as it is within budget!

However, we should explore some of the problems involved in post-mix processing.

Overall Compression

Compressing a complete mix reduces the difference between the quietest parts of the mix and the loudest. If the highest levels peak at around the same value as they did before compression then it follows that the average level must be higher, and this is reflected in a subjective increase in musical energy. However, a sound will only appear to be loud if it has a quieter sound with which to contrast, so there is a danger of making a piece of music sound quieter by compressing it too much.

When compressing a mix the attack time of the compressor is usually extended slightly to allow transient sounds, such as drums, to punch through with more power, though the best setting can only be determined by ear. It's also true that some compressors perform disappointingly when used on complete mixes, yet others produce results that appear to be little short of magic. As a general rule, soft-knee compressors produce the most subtle results – but do you always want to be subtle? Sadly, the compressors that work best in this situation also seem to cost the most! An important point is to choose a low ratio (1:1 to 1:5) and to set a low threshold (around −30dB).

Overall EQ

Equalising the whole mix might seem a little reckless but some equalisers seem to improve the sound noticeably, even when very subtle settings are used. Music can be made to appear louder by cutting the mid range slightly, as this emulates the response curve of the human ear. It may also be necessary to equalise a mix if it has been made in a studio with an inaccurate monitor system. Indeed, there are such a large number of inaccurate control rooms around that, when a master tape is sent to the cutting room to be prepared for record or CD mastering, it is very common for the engineer to apply a degree of corrective EQ at that stage.

Enhancers

It's not uncommon for whole mix to be treated with an exciter or a dynamic equaliser. These tend to emphasise certain parts of the frequency spectrum in a way that is related to the dynamics of the signal so that transient sounds are given more definition. This increases the perceived sense of loudness, which helps a record stand out from the competition on the radio or on the dance floor. The exciter actually synthesises harmonics based on the existing programme material, and so may be more suitable for dealing with an insufficiently bright mix. The dynamic equaliser creates no new harmonics, but instead redistributes those already present and so may give a smoother sound. Dynamic equalisers can also be used to add power at the bass end, whereas most exciters simply work at the very high-frequency end of the audio spectrum. Newer models, however, increasingly address the bottom end of the frequency spectrum by offering some type of bass enhancement.

Difficult Mixes

If you can't get a mix to sound right, checking the following points.

- Try to get a rough initial mix without using EQ or effects and then work from there. Also check that the mix sounds good in mono.

- Is the mix too busy? Do you need all those parts and, if so, can you afford to move some lower in the mix?

- Are mid-range sounds cluttering up the mix or overlapping with the bass sounds? If this is the case, try using EQ to thin out the sounds. They might sound odd in isolation, but they will probably sound right in the context of the whole mix. For example, shave some bottom end from a pad synth part or acoustic guitar rhythm line to clean up the low-mid region.

- If you're still having difficulty, balance up the drum and bass sounds first and then add the vocals and main instruments. You may find that the mix sounds 90% there with just drums, bass, chords and vocals.

- If you are working with a sequencer, try alternative pad or keyboard sounds if the sounds you have chosen appear to be taking up too much space.

- Use effects sparingly – add reverb where it sounds good, not simply where you feel it ought to be. Often the restrained use of effects produces the best results.

- Pan the instruments and effects to the desired places.

- There may be some benefit in adding a little compression to the complete mix, though this shouldn't be considered compulsory. A compressor with an auto attack/release feature may cope best with the shifting dynamics of a real mix, and a soft-knee expander will usually provide the most transparent results.

- Using tube compressors often gives the most flattering sound, and many of the top engineers like to pass the mix through their favourite tube compressor more for the benefit of the tube coloration than for the purposes of compression.

• Subtle use of an enhancer will also help separate the individual sounds and emphasise detail.

6 LIVE SOUND MIXING

Powered Mixers

Mixer amplifiers provide a convenient means of driving a small PA, and a number of more recent models also include digital reverb, which saves on the cost of external processor, reduces the amount of wiring to a bare minimum and also reduces the time it takes to set up the equipment. The obvious disadvantages are that, if there's a serious failure, you've lost both your power amps and your mixer, and if you want more power than is available you will have to buy external power amplifiers, which cancels out the advantage of compactness. However, it may be possible to switch the internal amplifiers to run your stage-monitor system, in which case adding external power amplifiers to drive the main PA is a sensible upgrade path. If you're intending to add sub-bass speakers at some stage, it's worth choosing one of the mixer amps that has an in-built active crossover (or the provision to fit one as an option) to cater for that eventuality. Powered mixers are limited, however, in that speaker cables tend to be longer due to the fact that they have to run all the way from the mixer to the speakers.

Practicalities

Acoustic feedback is the number one enemy in small venues, and the likelihood of experiencing feedback does not depend on how loud the system is running but rather on how much gain is being used. In other words, a loud singer working close to a microphone will be far less likely to encounter feedback problems than someone with a weak voice who doesn't keep close to the mic. There will always be some sound from the PA speakers that gets back into the vocal mics (even the pros can't prevent this entirely), but to keep it under control the system gain must be kept below the point at which feedback starts to build up. Unless you're miking quiet acoustic instruments, such as acoustic guitars, the most common source of feedback problems is the vocal mic setup, so that's the first area to check out.

The EQ settings needed to tame feedback will vary from system to system and venue to venue, as they will depend on the arrangements of the PA speakers, the monitor speakers, the mics and the positions of all of these components within the venue. The shape and size of the room also has a significant influence, as does the nature and position of any reflective surfaces. To reduce problems caused by feedback, you will need to 'ring out' the system.

Ringing Out

If you're using graphic equalisers, you'll need to ring out the system during the soundcheck and then apply cut in those frequency bands in which feedback is becoming a problem. The usual way to start is to have all of the EQ faders flat and then increase the system gain during the soundcheck until the feedback starts. Next, back off the level so that the system is just ringing when somebody speaks into a mic. Now you have to identify the frequency of this ring, which you can do by pulling down the faders one at a time. If nothing happens, return the fader to zero and repeat the process with the next one. Eventually you'll find one that makes the ringing stop. Pull this fader down by about 3dB and then slowly turn up the system gain until the ringing starts again. If it's at the same frequency, apply another 3dB of cut and continue with the process. Otherwise, identify the new ring frequency and pull that back by 3dB. If you don't have the experience to know roughly where the feedback is occurring then either a spectrum analyser or a graphic equaliser with feedback-detection LEDs on each band will help enormously. Repeat the process until all of the worst rings have been killed. Eventually you'll reach a point of diminishing returns at which no further adjustments help, or where you've moved the faders so far that the sound quality is starting to suffer. At this point call it a day and pull the overall PA level down about by 6dB from the level at which ringing occurs to restore stability.

The process of ringing out is necessary for both the main PA and the monitor system, and as you can imagine it takes both time and experience to perfect. As a rule, an automatic feedback reducer will perform more effectively, it will do the job in seconds rather than minutes, and it will have a far less obvious effect on the perceived sound thanks to the less intrusive nature of its very narrow filters.

Once you've set up the system EQ as best you can, turn up the gain until the ringing starts again and then back it off by around 10dB. This may seem like a long way, but if you stay to close to the feedback threshold the sound will continue to ring. What's more, you'll have virtually no scope for adjusting levels as the gig progresses. If you're lucky, when the audience come in the feedback threshold will rise by as much as 5dB purely because of sound being absorbed rather than reflected.

Some powered mixers come with five- or seven-band graphic equalisers built in. However, although these are useful for general tone shaping or for countering the worst anomalies of a room, they are too imprecise for controlling feedback or for precision room compensation. Ideally, a stereo 30-band third-octave equaliser should be used to exert more precise control.

Mixer Groups

Mixing a live gig can be quite a difficult task, so use the mixer to help you to simplify things. For example, if you have half a dozen drum mics around the kit, route those channels to a stereo group so that you can control the whole kit level using just one or two faders rather than six. Do the same for backing vocals, keyboards and any other sections where several sound sources need to be controlled without upsetting their relative levels.

Soundchecking

There comes a point when you've done all you can, and you have to make the best of what you have. Now is the time to start your soundcheck, and the first thing to do is to establish a safe maximum working vocal level. If you're really lucky this will be far too loud and you'll have to turn it down, but more often than not you'll have to run this near maximum to keep up with the rest of the band. However, it's best to pull back a few decibels from maximum so that you've got some power in hand if you need it. Always balance the back line to the vocal level and not vice versa. I've seen too many bands make the mistake of balancing the back-line first, and then, when they realise that the singer can't be heard above it, blaming the sound engineer!

Mixing Tips

Most types of music demand that the vocals are audible, so always make sure the vocals are sounding clear. If not, pull down the back-line level until you have a good balance. It is possible for the vocals to be too loud, but if you close your eyes and listen analytically then the performance should sound like a properly integrated whole, with no one part swamping out the rest.

After perfecting the vocals you will then need to get a good balance for the rhythm section, as this is the glue that holds the sound together. The drums and bass need to sit comfortably with each other, and if the drum sound is to boomy then you may need a touch of low-mid EQ cut to clean it up. If you can gate individual drums it can help a lot in keeping the sound clean, but if you haven't had much mixing experience I'd suggest that you leave this until you've got the hang of basic balancing.

I find it helpful to close my eyes from time to time when I'm listening as the visual impact of a show can completely change your perception of what's really going on. Keep notes on who takes the solos in which songs and where, as you'll probably need to boost their levels by a couple of decibels. You may also need to increase the effects levels for solos.

Pulling down the levels of mics in songs where they're not being used can help keep the sound clean, but make sure they're back on again when afterwards. If you're working with an unfamiliar band, pull unused mics down by 5–6dB rather than turning them off altogether so that, if somebody does suddenly start singing or playing, they won't be completely silent. This gives you a second or two to get their mic back to its normal level, and hopefully nobody will notice.

Concentration

Perhaps the most important element in mixing live sound is to keep your eye on the ball all the time. You shouldn't be constantly moving faders, but you'll probably need to move levels by around 3dB or so for solos, you'll need to cut mics that aren't being used, and you'll need to change effects patches as required. You must also make sure that you kill any vocal reverb between songs to keep the announcement clear and don't push it back up until the next song starts – performers have a habit of announcing a song and then coming back to say something else, and if the reverb is back up it sounds terrible.

Keep an ear open for creeping back-line levels, and if these cause a problem then ask the band to reset their levels as soon as there's a convenient break in the set. If you're not familiar with the band you can still tell a lot from body language, and with just a little practice you'll be able to tell who's about to play a solo and who's about to start singing.

Acoustic Music

Mixing folk music and ensembles in which the instruments are mainly acoustic is no more difficult than working with electric instruments, although, because of the potentially large number of mics that may be in use, you have to be very certain that you're working well below the feedback level. Sound will tend to leak from one mic to another, but that can sometimes help you because, if a mic is accidentally turned down when it's needed, the chances are that the performer will still be audible via the other mics, giving you time to reset the correct level. Provided that you make level changes slowly, no one will realise that you made a mistake!

Pay particular attention to the positioning of mics, as the closer the performers are to their mics the fewer feedback problems you will have and the better the overall separation will be. Watch during the performance for people moving out of range of their mics, and if necessary send a helper to move a mic back into place if the situation gets really difficult. Again, body language will tell you a lot about what's going on, as most players perform some kind of ritual before starting to play: wind players wet their reeds, fiddle players position their bows, percussionists pick up sticks and so on.

When two instruments are playing together, perhaps with one performing a harmonic counterpart to the other, ensure that they are reasonably balanced with each other. Close your eyes and confirm that both are clearly audible. Also, don't be afraid to drop the level of instruments if they are getting in the way of a vocal part or a lead instrument.

The Self-Op PA

If you're operating your own mix from on stage, balance it while one of your colleagues listens out at the front and then make as few changes as possible during the performance. Set up the mixer within arm's reach so that you can address any feedback problems simply by pulling down the master faders a touch. If any friends of the band who come to your gigs regularly have a good ear for balance, get them to report back on the sound during the show so that you can make changes if necessary. A few simple hand signals to indicate who's too loud and who's too quiet are all that's needed.

Common Problems

Without doubt, the most common problem in a live mix is being unable to get the vocal levels loud enough without experiencing feedback. However, it is essential when optimising your gain structure that you leave enough of a safety margin to push the vocal levels up during the gig, or you might find that distortion due to an overloading console becomes a problem before feedback does. If feedback really is the problem then your only course of action is to reduce the levels of the other band members, and you don't necessarily have to do this simply by pulling down level faders. Vocals occupy mainly the mid range of the audio spectrum, so by pulling some of the mid range out of the guitars and drums you should be able to increase the vocal clarity without robbing the overall mix of too much power. There's also the option of using an aural exciter or some other form of enhancer on the vocals to increase clarity without increasing level.

Room Boom

Booming is another common problem, especially in venues with poor acoustics. Assuming that you've done your best when positioning your speakers, make sure that all of the mics (except that for the kick drum) have their low-cut filters switched on, and if that doesn't work then try to identify the frequency at which the problem is at its worst and pull it down some more on your graphic EQ. As with feedback, the equalisation built into a typical live-sound console won't be adequate to perform this task properly. Before you even start, however, make sure it's not just an effect that occurs at your mixing position. Walk into the room and see if the problem is still as bad.

Anticipating Trouble

Modern equipment is very reliable, but it still breaks down from time to time. The most common casualties are leads, so check them regularly and always keep spares. In particular check all mains plugs, especially the tightness of the terminal screws holding the cable ends, and the cable clamp. It's also a good idea to carry a long mains extension lead for those occasions when the nearest power point is 30 feet away. Use one with a sufficient current rating and uncoil the cable completely, regardless of how much you actually need. If you draw a high current through a partially coiled mains cable it will get very hot, and I've seen them actually melt and catch fire!

Never trust the mains wiring at a venue. You can buy inexpensive devices that indicate the state of the mains, including the ground integrity, by means of a simple LED display. That said, it's also a very sensible move to use individual RCB trips (Residual Current Breakers) on the back-line amplification and on smaller PA systems so that, if a fault does occur in the middle of a performance, the power will shut off before anyone receives a lethal shock. Inexpensive units are available from garden suppliers for use with electrical garden tools.

GLOSSARY

AC
Alternating Current.

Active
Describes a circuit that contains transistors, ICs, tubes and other devices that require power to operate and are capable of amplification.

Active Sensing
System used to verify that a MIDI connection is working, in which the sending device frequently sends short messages to the receiving device to reassure it that all is well. If these active sensing messages stop for any reason, the receiving device will recognise a fault condition and switch off all notes. Not all MIDI devices support active sensing.

A/D Converter
Circuit for converting analogue waveforms into a series of values represented by binary numbers. The more bits a converter has, the greater the resolution of the

sampling process. Current effects units are generally 16 bits or more, with the better models being either 20- or 24-bit.

AFL
After-Fade Listen, a system used within mixing consoles to allow specific signals to be monitored at the level set by their fader or level control knob. Aux sends are generally monitored AFL rather than PFL so that the actual signal being fed to an effects unit can be monitored.

Algorithm
Computer program designed to perform a specific task. In the context of effects units, algorithms usually describe a software building block designed to create a specific effect or combination of effects. All digital effects are based on algorithms.

Ambience
The result of sound reflections in a confined space being added to the original sound. Ambience may also be created electronically by some digital reverb units. The main difference between ambience and reverberation is that ambience doesn't have the characteristic long delay time of reverberation – the reflections mainly give the sound a sense of space.

Amp

Unit of electrical current, short for ampere.

Amplifier

Device that increases the level of an electrical signal.

Amplitude

Another word for level. Can refer to levels of sound or electrical signal.

Analogue

Circuitry that uses a continually changing voltage or current to represent a signal. The origin of the term is that the electrical signal can be thought of as being analogous to the original signal.

ASCII

American Standard Code for Information Interchange. A standard code for representing computer keyboard characters with binary data.

Attack

Time taken for a sound to achieve maximum amplitude. Drums have a fast attack, whereas bowed strings have a slow attack. In compressors and gates, the attack time equates to how quickly the processor can change its gain.

Attenuate
To make lower in level.

Audio Frequency
Signals in the human audio range, nominally between 20Hz and 20kHz.

Aux
Control on a mixing console designed to route a proportion of the channel signal to the effects or cue mix outputs. (See *Aux Send*.)

Aux Return
Mixer inputs used to add effects to the mix.

Aux Send
Physical output from a mixer aux send buss.

Balance
This word has several meanings in recording. It may refer to the relative levels of the left and right channels of a stereo recording, or it may be used to describe the relative levels of the various instruments and voices within a mix.

Balanced Wiring
Wiring system which uses two out-of-phase conductors

and a common screen to reduce the effect of interference. For balancing to be effective, both the sending and receiving device must have balanced output and input stages respectively.

Bandpass
Filter that passes frequencies only between specific upper and lower limits.

Bandpass Filter
Filter that removes or attenuates frequencies above and below the frequency at which it is set. Frequencies within the band are emphasised. Bandpass filters are often used in synthesisers as tone-shaping elements.

Bandwidth
Means of specifying the range of frequencies passed by an electronic circuit such as an amplifier, mixer or filter. The frequency range is usually measured at the points where the level drops by 3dB relative to the maximum.

Binary
Counting system based on only two numbers: 1 and 0.

Bit
Binary digit, which may either be 1 or 0.

Boost/Cut Control

single control which allows the range of frequencies passing through a filter to be either amplified or attenuated. The centre position is usually the 'flat' or 'no effect' position.

BPM

Beats Per Minute.

Breath Controller

Device that converts breath pressure into MIDI controller data.

Buffer

Circuit designed to isolate the output of a source device from loading effects due to the input impedance of the destination device.

Buffer Memory

Temporary RAM memory used in some computer operations, sometimes to prevent a break in the data stream when the computer is interrupted to perform another task.

Bug

Slang term for software fault or equipment design problem.

Buss

Common electrical signal path along which signals may travel. In a mixer, there are several busses carrying the stereo mix, the groups, the PFL signal, the aux sends and so on. Power supplies are also fed along busses.

Byte

Piece of digital data comprising eight bits.

Cardioid

Meaning 'heart-shaped', describes the polar response of a unidirectional microphone.

Channel

In the context of MIDI, Channel refers to one of 16 possible data channels over which MIDI data may be sent. The organisation of data by channels means that up to 16 different MIDI instruments or parts may be addressed using a single cable.

Channel

In the context of mixing consoles, a channel is a single strip of controls relating to one input.

Chase

Term describing the process whereby a slave device attempts to synchronise itself with a master device. In the context of a MIDI sequence, Chase may also involve chasing events – looking back to earlier positions in the song to see if there are any program changes or other events that need to be acted upon.

Chord
Two or more different musical notes played at the same time.

Chorus
Effect created by doubling a signal and adding delay and pitch modulation.

Chromatic
Scale of pitches rising in steps of one semitone.

Click Track
Metronome pulse which helps musicians to keep time.

Clipping
Severe form of distortion which occurs when a signal attempts to exceed the maximum level which a piece of equipment can handle.

Common-Mode Rejection
Measure of how well a balanced circuit rejects a signal that is common to both inputs.

Compander

Encode/decode device that compresses a signal while encoding it, then expands it when decoding it.

Compressor

Device designed to reduce the dynamic range of audio signals by reducing the level of high signals or by increasing the level of low signals.

Conductor

Material that provides low resistance for electrical current.

Console

Alternative term for mixer.

Contact Enhancer

Compound designed to increase the electrical conductivity of electrical contacts such as plugs, sockets and edge connectors.

Continuous Controller

MIDI message used to translate continuous change, such as from a pedal, wheel or breath control device.

Copy Protection

Method used by software manufacturers to prevent unauthorised copying.

Crash

Slang term relating to malfunction of a computer program.

Cut-And-Paste Editing

Copying or moving sections of a recording to different locations.

Cutoff Frequency

Frequency above or below which attenuation begins in a filter circuit.

Cycle

A complete vibration of a sound source or its electrical equivalent. One cycle per second is known as 1Hz (Hertz).

CV

Control Voltage. Used to control the pitch of an oscillator or filter frequency in an analogue synthesiser. Most analogue synthesisers follow a one volt per octave convention, though there are exceptions. To use a pre-MIDI analogue synthesiser under MIDI control, a MIDI-to-CV converter is required.

Daisy Chain

Term used to describe serial electrical connection between devices or modules.

Damping

In the context of reverberation, damping refers to the rate at which reverberant energy is absorbed by the various surfaces in an environment.

DAT

Abbreviation of Digital Audio Tape. The most commonly used DAT machines are more correctly known as R-DATs because they use a rotating head similar to that in a video recorder. Digital recorders using fixed or stationary heads (such as DCC) are known as S-DAT machines.

Data

Information stored and used by a computer.

Data Compression

System for reducing the amount of data stored by a digital system. Most audio data compression systems are known as *lossy* systems, as some of the original signal is discarded in accordance with psychoacoustic principles designed to ensure that only components which cannot be heard are lost.

dB

Decibel. Unit used to express the relative levels of two electrical voltages, powers or sounds.

dBm
Variation on dB referenced to odB = 1mW into 600 ohms.

dBv
Variation on dB referenced to odB = 0.775v.

dBV
Variation on dB referenced to odB = 1V.

dB Per Octave
A means of measuring the slope of a filter. The more decibels per octave the sharper the filter slope.

dbx
A commercial encode/decode tape noise-reduction system that operates by compressing the signal during recording and expands it by an identical amount on playback.

DC
Direct Current.

DCC
Stationary-head digital recorder format developed by Philips. Uses a data-compression system to reduce the amount of data that needs to be stored.

DCO
Digitally Controlled Oscillator.

DDL
Digital Delay Line.

Decay
Progressive reduction in amplitude of a sound or electrical signal over time. In the context of an ADSR envelope shaper, the decay phase starts as soon as the attack phase has reached its maximum level. In the decay phase, the signal level drops until it reaches the sustain level set by the user. The signal then remains at this level until the key is released, at which point the release phase is entered.

De-esser
Device for reducing the effect of sibilance in vocal signals.

Defragmentation
Process of rearranging the files on a hard disk so that all of the files are as contiguous as possible, and that the remaining free space is also contiguous.

Deoxidising Compound
Substance formulated to remove oxides from electrical contacts.

Detent
Physical click stop in the centre of a control such as a pan or EQ cut/boost knob.

DI
Direct Inject, in which a signal is plugged directly into an audio chain without the aid of a microphone.

DI Box
Device for matching the signal-level impedance of a source to a tape machine or mixer input.

Digital
Describes an electronic system which represents data and signals in the form of codes comprising 1s and 0s.

Digital Delay
Digital processor designed for generating delay and echo effects.

Digital Reverb
Digital processor for simulating reverberation.

DIN Connector
Consumer multi-pin signal connection format, also used for MIDI cabling. Various pin configurations are available.

Direct Coupling
Means of connecting two electrical circuits so that both AC and DC signals may be passed between them.

Disc
Used to describe vinyl discs, CDs and MiniDiscs.

Disk
Abbreviation of *diskette*, but now used to describe computer floppy, hard and removable disks. (See *Floppy Disk*.)

Dither
System of adding low-level noise to a digitised audio signal in a way that extends the low-level resolution at the expense of a slight deterioration in noise performance.

DMA
Direct Memory Access. Part of a computer operating system that allows peripheral devices to communicate directly with the computer memory without going via the CPU (Central Processing Unit).

Dolby
An encode/decode tape noise reduction system that amplifies low-level, high-frequency signals during recording, then reverses this process during playback.

There are several different Dolby systems in use, including types B, C and S for domestic and semi-professional machines, and types A and SR for professional machines. Recordings made whilst using one of these systems must also be replayed via the same system.

DOS
Disk Operating System. Part of the operating system of PC and PC-compatible computers.

Driver
Piece of software that handles communications between the main program and a hardware peripheral, such as a soundcard, printer or scanner.

Drum Pad
Synthetic playing surface which produces electronic trigger signals in response to being hit with drumsticks.

Dry
Signal to which no effects have been added. Conversely, a sound which has been treated with an effect, such as reverberation, is referred to as wet.

DSP
Digital Signal Processor. A powerful microchip used to process digital signals.

Dubbing

Adding further material to an existing recording. Also known as *overdubbing*.

Ducking

System for controlling the level of one audio signal with another. For example, background music can be made to duck whenever there is a voice-over.

Dump

To transfer digital data from one device to another. A Sysex dump is a means of transmitting information about a particular instrument or module over MIDI, and may be used to store sound patches, parameter settings and so on.

Dynamic Microphone

Type of microphone that works on the electric generator principle, whereby a diaphragm moves a coil of wire within a magnetic field.

Dynamic Range

Range in decibels between the highest signal that can be handled by a piece of equipment and the level at which small signals disappear into the noise floor.

Dynamics

Method of describing the relative levels within a piece of music.

Early Reflections
First sound reflections from walls, floors and ceilings following a sound which is created in an acoustically reflective environment.

Effects Loop
Connection system that allows an external signal processor to be connected into the audio chain.

Effects Return
Additional mixer input designed to accommodate the output from an effects unit.

Effects Unit
Device for treating an audio signal in order to change it in some way. Effects often involve the use of delay circuits, and include such treatments as reverb and echo.

Encode/Decode
System that requires a signal to be processed prior to recording, which is then reversed during playback.

Enhancer
Device designed to brighten audio material using

techniques such as dynamic equalisation, phase shifting and harmonic generation.

Envelope
The way in which the level of a sound or signal varies over time.

Envelope Generator
Circuit capable of generating a control signal which represents the envelope of the sound you want to recreate. This may then be used to control the level of an oscillator or other sound source, though envelopes may also be used to control filter or modulation settings. The most common example is the ADSR generator.

Equaliser
Device for selectively cutting or boosting selected parts of the audio spectrum.

Erase
To remove recorded material from an analogue tape, or to remove digital data from any form of storage medium.

Event
In MIDI terms, an event is a single unit of MIDI data, such as a note being turned on or off, a piece of controller information, a program change, and so on.

Exciter
Enhancer that works by synthesising new high-frequency harmonics.

Expander
Device designed to decrease the level of low-level signals and increase the level of high-level signals, thus increasing the dynamic range of the signal.

Expander Module
Synthesiser with no keyboard, often rack mountable or in some other compact format.

Fader
Sliding potentiometer control used in mixers and other processors.

FET
Field Effect Transistor.

Figure Of Eight
Describes the polar response of a microphone that is equally sensitive at both front and rear, yet rejects sounds coming from the sides.

File
Meaningful list of data stored in digitally. A Standard

MIDI File is a specific type of file designed to allow sequence information to be exchanged between different types of sequencer.

Filter
Electronic circuit designed to emphasise or attenuate a specific range of frequencies.

Flanging
Modulated delay effect using feedback to create a dramatic, sweeping sound.

Floppy Disk
Computer disk that uses a flexible magnetic medium encased in a protective plastic sleeve. The maximum capacity of a standard high-density disk is 1.44Mb. Earlier double-density disks hold only around half the amount of data.

Flutter Echo
Resonant echo that occurs when sound reflects back and forth between two parallel reflective surfaces.

Foldback
System for feeding one or more separate mixes to the performers for use while recording and overdubbing. Also known as a *cue mix*.

Formant

Frequency component or resonance of an instrument or voice sound that doesn't change with the pitch of the note being played or sung. For example, the body resonance of an acoustic guitar remains constant regardless of the note being played.

Format

Procedure required to ready a computer disk for use. Formatting organises the disk's surface into a series of electronic pigeonholes into which data can be stored. Different computers often use different formatting systems.

Fragmentation

Process by which the available space on a disk drive is split up into small sections due to the storing and erasing of files. (See *Defragmentation*.)

Frequency

Indication of how many cycles of a repetitive waveform occur in one second. A waveform which has a repetition cycle of once per second has a frequency of 1Hz.

Frequency Response

Measurement of the frequency range that can be handled by a specific piece of electrical equipment or loudspeaker.

FSK
Frequency-Shift Keying, a method of recording a sync clock signal onto tape by representing it as two alternating tones.

Fundamental
Any sound comprises a fundamental or basic frequency plus harmonics and partials at a higher frequency.

FX
Shorthand for effects.

Gain
Amount by which a circuit amplifies a signal.

Gate
Electrical signal that is generated whenever a key is depressed on an electronic keyboard. This is used to trigger envelope generators and other events that need to be synchronised to key action.

Gate
Electronic device designed to mute low-level signals, improving the noise performance during pauses in the wanted material.

General MIDI

Addition to the basic MIDI spec to assure a minimum level of compatibility when playing back GM-format song files. The specification covers type and program, number of sounds, minimum levels of polyphony and multitimbrality, response to controller information and so on.

Glitch
Describes an unwanted short-term corruption of a signal, or the unexplained short-term malfunction of a piece of equipment. For example, an inexplicable click on a DAT tape would be termed a glitch.

GM Reset
Universal Sysex command which activates the General MIDI mode on a GM instrument. The same command also sets all controllers to their default values and switches off any notes still playing by means of an All Notes Off message.

Graphic Equaliser
Equaliser on which several narrow segments of the audio spectrum are controlled by individual cut/boost faders. The name derives from the fact that the fader positions provide a graphic representation of the EQ curve.

Ground

Electrical earth, or zero volts. In mains wiring, the ground cable is physically connected to the ground via a long conductive metal spike.

Ground Loops

Also known as *earth loops*. Wiring problems in which currents circulate in the ground wiring of an audio system, known as the *ground-loop effect*. When these currents are induced by the alternating mains supply, hum results.

Group

Collection of signals within a mixer that are mixed and then routed through a separate fader to provide overall control. In a multitrack mixer, several groups are provided to feed the various recorder track inputs.

GS

Roland's own extension to the General MIDI protocol.

Hard Disk

High-capacity computer storage device based on a rotating rigid disk with a magnetic coating onto which data may be recorded.

Harmonic

High-frequency component of a complex waveform.

Harmonic Distortion
Addition of harmonics that aren't present in the original signal.

Head
Part of a tape machine or disk drive that reads and/or writes data to and from the storage media.

Headroom
The safety margin in decibels between the highest peak signal being passed by a piece of equipment and the absolute maximum level the equipment can handle.

High-Pass Filter
Filter which attenuates frequencies below its cutoff frequency.

Hiss
Noise caused by random electrical fluctuations.

Hum
Signal contamination caused by the addition of low frequencies, usually related to the mains power frequency.

Hz
Shorthand for Hertz, the unit of frequency.

IC

Integrated Circuit.

Impedance

Can be visualised as the AC resistance of a circuit which contains both resistive and reactive components.

Inductor

Reactive component which presents an impedance with increases with frequency.

Initialise

To automatically restore a piece of equipment to its factory default settings.

Insert Point

Connector that allows an external processor to be patched into a signal path so that the signal then flows through the external processor.

Insulator

Material that does not conduct electricity.

Intermittent

Usually describes a fault that only appears occasionally.

Intermodulation Distortion

Form of distortion that introduces frequencies not present in the original signal. These are invariably based on the sum and difference products of the original frequencies.

I/O
The part of a system that handles inputs and outputs, usually in the digital domain.

IPS
Inches Per Second. Used to describe tape speed.

IRQ
Interrupt Request. Part of the operating system of a computer that allows a connected device to request attention from the processor in order to transfer data to it or from it.

Jack
Commonly used audio connector, mono (TS) or stereo (TRS).

k
Abbreviation for 1,000 (kilo). Used as a prefix to other values to indicate magnitude.

LCD
Liquid Crystal Display.

LED

Light-Emitting Diode, a solid-state lamp.

LSB

Least Significant Byte. If a piece of data has to be conveyed as two bytes, one byte represents high-value numbers and the other low-value numbers, in much the same way as tens and units function in the decimal system. The high value, or most significant part of the message, is called the MSB (Most Significant Byte).

Limiter

Device that controls the gain of a signal so as to prevent it from ever exceeding a preset level. Essentially, a rapidly acting compressor with an infinite compression ratio.

Linear

Describes a device where the output is a direct multiple of the input.

Line Level

Mixers and signal processors tend to work at a standard signal level known as line level. In practice there are several different standard line levels, but all are in the order of a few volts. A nominal signal level is around −10dBv for semi-pro equipment and +4dBv for professional equipment.

Load

Electrical circuit that draws power from another circuit or power supply. Also describes reading data into a computer.

Load On/Off

Function to allow the keyboard and sound-generating section of a keyboard synthesiser to be used independently of each other.

Logic

Type of electronic circuitry used for processing binary signals comprising two discrete voltage levels.

Loop

Circuit in which the output is connected back to the input.

Low-Frequency Oscillator

Oscillator used as a modulation source, usually below 20Hz. The most common LFO waveshape is the sine wave, though there is often a choice of sine, square, triangular and sawtooth waveforms.

Low-Pass Filter

A filter which attenuates frequencies above its cutoff frequency.

mA

Milliamp, or one thousandth of an amp.

MDM

Modular Digital Multitrack, a digital recorder that can be used in multiples to provide a greater number of synchronised tracks than a single machine.

Memory

Computer's RAM memory used to store programs and data. This data is lost when the computer is switched off and so must be stored to disk or other suitable media.

Menu

List of choices presented by a computer program or a device with a display window.

Mic Level

Low-level signal generated by a microphone. This must be amplified many times to increase it to line level.

Microprocessor

Specialised microchip at the heart of a computer. It is here that instructions are read and acted upon.

MIDI

Musical Instrument Digital Interface.

MIDI Analyser
Device that gives a visual readout of MIDI activity when connected between two pieces of MIDI equipment.

MIDI Bank Change
Type of controller message used to select alternate banks of MIDI programs where access to more than 128 programs is required.

MIDI Controller
Term used to describe the physical interface by means of which the musician plays the MIDI synthesiser or other sound generator. Examples of controllers are keyboards, drum pads, wind synths and so on.

MIDI Control Change
Also known as *MIDI controllers* or *controller data*. These messages convey positional information relating to performance controls such as wheels, pedals, switches and other devices. This information can be used to control functions such as vibrato depth, brightness, portamento, effects levels, and many other parameters.

(Standard) MIDI File
Standard file format for storing song data recorded on a MIDI sequencer in such as way as to allow it to be read by other makes or models of MIDI sequencer.

MIDI Implementation Chart

A chart, usually found in MIDI product manuals, which provides information as to which MIDI features are supported. Supported features are marked with a o while unsupported feature are marked with a X. Additional information may be provided, such as the exact form of the bank change message.

MIDI In

The socket used to receive information from a master controller or from the MIDI Thru socket of a slave unit.

MIDI Merge

Device or sequencer function that enables two or more streams of MIDI data to be combined.

MIDI Mode

MIDI information can be interpreted by the receiving MIDI instrument in a number of ways, the most common being polyphonically on a single MIDI channel (Poly [Omni Off] mode). Omni mode enables a MIDI Instrument to play all incoming data regardless of channel.

MIDI Module

Sound-generating device with no integral keyboard.

MIDI Note Number

Every key on a MIDI keyboard has its own note number, ranging from 0 to 127, where 60 represents middle C. Some systems use C3 as middle C while others use C4.

MIDI Note Off
MIDI message sent when key is released.

MIDI Note On
Message sent when note is pressed.

MIDI Out
MIDI connector used to send data from a master device to the MIDI In of a connected slave device.

MIDI Port
MIDI connections of a MIDI-compatible device. A multiport, in the context of a MIDI interface, is a device with multiple MIDI output sockets, each capable of carrying data relating to a different set of 16 MIDI channels. Multiports are the only means of exceeding the limitations imposed by 16 MIDI channels.

MIDI Program Change
Type of MIDI message used to change sound patches on a remote module or the effects patch on a MIDI effects unit.

MIDI Sync
Description of the synchronisation systems available to MIDI users: MIDI Clock and MIDI Time Code.

MIDI Thru
Socket on a slave unit used to feed the MIDI In socket of the next unit in line.

MIDI Thru Box
Device which splits the MIDI Out signal of a master instrument or sequencer to avoid daisy chaining. Powered circuitry is used to 'buffer' the outputs so as to prevent problems when many pieces of equipment are driven from a single MIDI output.

Mixer
Device for combining two or more audio signals.

Monitor
Reference loudspeaker used for mixing.

Monitor
VDU for a computer.

Monitoring
Action of listening to a mix or to a specific audio signal.

Monophonic
One note at a time.

MTC
MIDI Time Code. A MIDI sync implementation based on SMPTE timecode.

Multisampling
Creation of several samples, each covering a limited musical range, the idea being to produce a more natural range of sounds across the range of the instrument being sampled. For example, a piano may need to be sampled every two or three semitones in order to sound convincing.

Multitimbral Module
MIDI sound source capable of producing several different sounds at the same time and controlled on different MIDI channels.

Multitrack
Device capable of recording several 'parallel' parts or tracks which may then be mixed or re-recorded independently.

Near Field
Some people prefer the term 'close field' to describe a loudspeaker system designed to be used close to the

listener. The advantage is that the listener hears more of the direct sound from the speakers and less of the reflected sound from the room.

Noise Reduction

System for reducing analogue tape noise or for reducing the level of hiss present in a recording.

Noise Shaping

System for creating digital dither so that any added noise is shifted into those parts of the audio spectrum where the human ear is least sensitive.

Non-Linear

Describes digital recording systems that allow any parts of the recording to be played back in any order with no gaps. Conventional tape is referred to as linear, because the material can only play back in the order in which it was recorded.

Non-Registered Parameter Number

Addition to the basic MIDI spec that allows controllers 98 and 99 to be used to control non-standard parameters relating to particular models of synthesiser. This is an alternative to using system-exclusive data to achieve the same ends, though NRPNs tend to be used mainly by Yamaha and Roland instruments.

Normalise
A socket is said to be normalised when it is wired so that the original signal path is maintained, unless a plug is inserted. The most common examples of normalised connectors are the insert points on a mixing console.

Octave
When a frequency or pitch is transposed up by one octave, its frequency is doubled.

Offline
Describes a process carried out while a recording is not playing. For example, some computer-based processes have to be carried out off-line as the computer isn't fast enough to carry out the process in real time.

Ohm
Unit of electrical resistance.

Omni
Refers to a microphone that is equally sensitive in all directions, or to the MIDI mode in which data on all channels is recognised.

Open Circuit
Break in an electrical circuit that prevents current from flowing.

Open Reel

Tape machine on which the tape is wound on spools rather than sealed in a cassette.

Operating System

Basic software that enables a computer to load and run other programs.

Opto-Electronic Device

Device on which some electrical parameters change in response to a variation in light intensity. Variable photoresistors are sometimes used as gain control elements in compressors where the side-chain signal modulates the light intensity.

Oscillator

Circuit that generates a periodic electrical waveform.

Overdub

To add another part to a multitrack recording or to replace one of the existing parts. (See *Dubbing*.)

Overload

To exceed the operating capacity of an electronic or electrical circuit.

Pan Pot

Control enabling the user of a mixer to move the signal to any point in the stereo soundstage by varying the relative levels fed to the left and right stereo outputs.

Parallel
Method of connecting two or more circuits together so that their inputs and outputs are all connected together.

Parameter
Variable value that affects some aspect of a device's performance.

Parametric EQ
Equaliser with separate controls for frequency, bandwidth and cut/boost.

Passive
Circuit with no active elements.

Patch
Alternative term for program. Referring to a single programmed sound within a synthesiser that can be called up using program-change commands. MIDI effects units and samplers also have patches.

Patch Bay
System of panel-mounted connectors used to bring

inputs and outputs to a central point from where they can be routed using plug-in patch cords.

Patch Cord
Short cable used with patch bays.

Peak
Maximum instantaneous level of a signal.

Peak
The highest signal level in any section of programme material.

PFL
Pre-Fade Listen. A system used within a mixing console to allow the operator to listen in on a selected signal, regardless of the position of the fader controlling that signal.

Phantom Power
48V DC supply for capacitor microphones, transmitted along the signal cores of a balanced mic cable.

Phase
Timing difference between two electrical waveforms expressed in degrees where 360º corresponds to a delay of exactly one cycle.

Phaser

Effect which combines a signal with a phase-shifted version of itself to produce creative filtering effects. Most phasers are controlled by means of an LFO.

Phono Plug

Hi-fi connector developed by RCA and used extensively on semi-pro, unbalanced recording equipment.

Pickup

Part of a guitar that converts string vibrations to electrical signals.

Pitch

Musical interpretation of an audio frequency.

Pitch Bend

Special control message designed specifically to produce a change in pitch in response to the movement of a pitch bend wheel or lever. Pitch bend data can be recorded and edited, just like any other MIDI controller data, even though it isn't part of the controller message group.

Pitch Shifter

Device for changing the pitch of an audio signal without changing its duration.

Polyphony

An instrument's ability to play two or more notes simultaneously. An instrument which can play only one note at a time is described as monophonic.

Port

Connection for the input or output of data.

Portamento

Gliding effect that allows a sound to change pitch at a gradual rate rather than abruptly when a new key is pressed or MIDI note sent.

Post-Production

Work performed on a stereo recording after mixing has been completed.

Post-Fade

Aux signal taken from after the channel fader so that the aux send level follows any channel fader changes. Normally used for feeding effects devices.

PPM

Peak Programme Meter. A meter designed to register signal peaks rather than the average level.

Pre-Fade

Aux signal taken from before the channel fader so that the channel fader has no effect on the aux send level. Normally used for creating foldback or cue mixes.

Preset

Effects unit or synth patch that cannot be altered by the user.

Processor

Device designed to treat an audio signal by changing its dynamics or frequency content. Examples of processors include compressors, gates and equalisers.

Punching In

Action of placing an already recorded track into record at the correct time during playback so that the existing material may be extended or replaced.

Punching Out

Action of switching a tape machine (or other recording device) out of Record after executing a punch-in. With most multitrack machines, both punching in and punching out can be accomplished without stopping the tape.

PZM

Pressure Zone Microphone, a type of boundary mic

designed to reject out-of-phase sounds reflected from surfaces within the recording environment.

Q

Measurement of the resonant properties of a filter. The higher the Q, the more resonant the filter and the narrower the range of frequencies that are allowed to pass.

Quantising

Means of moving notes recorded in a MIDI sequencer so that they line up with user defined subdivisions of a musical bar – 16s, for example. The facility may be used to correct timing errors, but over-quantising can remove the human feel from a performance.

R-DAT

Digital tape machine using a rotating head system.

Real Time

Audio process that can be carried out as the signal is being recorded or played back. The opposite is off-line, where the signal is processed in non-real time.

Release

Time taken for a level or gain to return to normal. Often used to describe the rate at which a synthesised sound reduces in level after a key has been released.

Resistance
Opposition to the flow of electrical current. Measured in ohms.

Resolution
Accuracy with which an analogue signal is represented by a digitising system. The more bits are used, the more accurately the amplitude of each sample can be measured, but there are other elements of converter design that also affect accuracy. High conversion accuracy is known as *high resolution*.

Resonance
Same as Q.

Reverb
Acoustic ambience created by multiple reflections in a confined space.

RF
Radio Frequency.

RF Interference
Interference significantly above the human hearing range.

ribbon microphone
Microphone in which the sound-capturing element is a

thin metal ribbon suspended in a magnetic filed. When sound causes the ribbon to vibrate, a small electrical current is generated within the ribbon.

Release
Rate at which a signal amplitude decays once a key has been released.

Resonance
Characteristic of a filter that allows it to selectively pass a narrow range of frequencies. (See Q.)

RMS
Root Mean Square, a method of specifying the behaviour of a piece of electrical equipment under continuous sine wave testing conditions.

Roll-off
The rate at which a filter attenuates a signal once it has passed the filter cutoff point.

ROM
Abbreviation for Read-Only Memory. This is a permanent and non-volatile type of memory containing data that can't be changed. Operating systems are often stored on ROM as the memory remains intact when the power is switched off.

Sample
Process carried out by an A/D converter where the instantaneous amplitude of a signal is measured many times per second (44.1kHz in the case of CD).

Sample
Digitised sound used as a musical sound source in a sampler or additive synthesiser.

Sample And Hold
Usually refers to a feature whereby random values are generated at regular intervals and then used to control another function such as pitch or filter frequency. Sample and hold circuits were also used in old analogue synthesisers to 'remember' the note being played after a key had been released.

Sample Rate
Number of times which an A/D converter samples the incoming waveform each second.

Sequencer
Device for recording and replaying MIDI data, usually in a multitrack format, allowing complex compositions to be built up a part at a time.

Short Circuit

Low-resistance path that allows electrical current to flow. The term is usually used to describe a current path that exists through a faulty condition.

Sibilance
High-frequency whistling or lisping sound that affects vocal recordings due either to poor mic technique or excessive equalisation.

Side Chain
Part of a circuit that splits off a proportion of the main signal to be processed in some way. Compressors uses aside-chain signal to derive their control signals.

Signal
Electrical representation of input such as sound.

Signal Chain
Route taken by a signal from the input of a system to its output.

Signal-To-Noise Ratio
Ratio of maximum signal level to the residual noise, expressed in decibels.

Single-Ended Noise Reduction
Device for removing or attenuating the noise component

of a signal. Doesn't require previous coding, as in the case of Dolby or dbx.

SMPTE
Timecode developed by the Society Of Motion Picture And Television Engineers but now extensively used in music and recording. SMPTE is a real-time code and is related to hours, minutes, seconds and film or video frames rather than to musical tempo.

SPL
Sound-Pressure Level, measured in decibels.

Stereo
Two-channel system feeding left and right loudspeakers.

Sub-Bass
Frequencies below the range of typical monitor loudspeakers. Some define sub-bass as frequencies that can be felt rather than heard.

Sustain
Part of the ADSR envelope which determines the level to which the sound will settle if a key is held down. Once the key is released, the sound decays at a rate set by the release parameter. Also refers to a guitar's ability to hold notes which decay very slowly.

Sweet Spot

Optimum position for a microphone or a listener relative to monitor loudspeakers.

Sync

System for making two or more pieces of equipment run in synchronism with each other.

Synthesiser

Electronic musical instrument designed to create a wide range of sounds, both imitative and abstract.

Tape Head

Part of a tape machine that transfers magnetic energy to the tape during recording or reads it during playback.

Tempo

Rate of the beat of a piece of music, measured here in beats per minute.

Test Tone

Steady, fixed-level tone recorded onto a multitrack or stereo recording to act as a reference when matching levels.

Timbre

Tonal 'colour' of a sound.

Track

This term dates back to multitrack tape, on which the tracks are physical stripes of recorded material located side by side along the length of the tape.

Tracking

System whereby one device follows another. Tracking is often discussed in the context of MIDI guitar synthesisers or controllers where the MIDI output attempts to track the pitch of the guitar strings.

Transparency

Subjective term used to describe audio quality where the high-frequency detail is clear and individual sounds are easy to identify and separate.

Transpose

To shift a musical signal by a fixed number of semitones.

Tremolo

Modulation of the amplitude of a sound using an low-frequency oscillator.

TRS Jack

Stereo-type jack with tip, ring and sleeve connections.

Unbalanced

Describes a two-wire electrical signal connection in which the inner (hot or positive) conductor is usually surrounded by the cold (negative) conductor, forming a screen against interference.

Unison
To play the same melody using two or more different instruments or voices.

Velocity
The rate at which a key is depressed. This may be used to control loudness (to simulate the response of instruments) or other parameters on later synths.

Vibrato
Pitch modulation using a low-frequency oscillator to modulate a voltage-controlled oscillator.

Voice
Capacity of a synthesiser to play a single musical note. An instrument capable of playing 16 simultaneous notes is said to be a 16-voice instrument.

Volt
Unit of electrical power.

VU Meter

Meter designed to interpret signal levels in roughly the same way as the human ear, which responds more closely to the average levels of sounds rather than to the peak levels.

Watt
Unit of electrical power.

White Noise
Random signal with an energy distribution that produces the same amount of noise power per Hz.

XLR
Type of connector commonly used to carry balanced audio signals including, the feeds from microphones.

Y-Lead
Lead split so that one source can feed two destinations. Y-leads may also be used in console insert points, when a stereo jack plug at one end of the lead is split into two monos at the other.